"CNEOPSA Project.......the first attempt to deal systematically with ethnic minorities and dementia"
- *Mr. Lars Rasmussen in the Forewords*

"It is one thing to describe, another to suggest concrete action. The authors in this book have taken the bold step to recommend a comprehensive strategy in research, training of professionals, information programme aimed at minority ethnic families and support to minority ethnic organisations. The UK proposal of a satellite model in building specialist organisations in dementia care is to be welcomed. What remains now is for all the relevant players in dementia care to make this possible from policymakers, planners, researchers, professionals and minority ethnic groups."
- *Sir Herman Ouseley, Chairman, Commission for Racial Equality*

"The more we learn about dementia - the more questions seem to appear...in learning about the improvement of professional care and support to ethnic minority families. We begin to see how, not only the brain damaging, but rather social and cultural aspects determine their everyday life. This guide takes us closer to an understanding of 'people with Alzheimer's Disease' not as group, but as very different people.".
- *Dr.Christine E. Swane, Acting Director, Danish Institute of Gerontology.*

"This book from the *CNEOPSA* Project breaks new ground. It does not take the easy route of mere description. Instead it provides country details in full with recommendations on the nature of country practice for policymakers, professionals and organisations. The contents of this book cannot be ignored since much needs to be done given the low knowledge and practice base as the authors point out. We in the Alzheimer's Disease Society will play our part in helping the goal of appropriate dementia care to minority ethnic older people in the UK."
- *Mr. Brian Roycroft CBE, Chairperson, Alzheimer's Disease Society*

"In its subtle and sensitive findings this report begins to set the agenda for the further work which is urgently required"
- *Professor Mary Marshall in the Forewords*

3

Contents

Dementia and Minority Ethnic Older People

Managing Care in the UK, Denmark and Franc

Naina Patel and Naheed Mirza [UK]

Peter Lindblad and Kirsten Amstrup [Denmark]

Omar Samaoli [France]

 **Russell House Publishing Ltd**

First published in 1998 by

Russell House Publishing Ltd.
4 St.George's House,
The Business Park
Uplyme Road,
Lyme Regis,
DT7 3LS,
UK

© 1998 Naina Patel, Naheed Mirza, Peter Lindblad, Kirsten Amstrup, Omar Samaoli

British Library Cataloguing-in-Publication Data:
A catalogue record for this book is available from the British Library.
ISBN 1-898924-33-3

Design by Paul Morton (cover) and Jessie Bura (text), Hot Frog Graphics, Barnsley.

Printed by Mercury Print & Packaging, The Print Factory, Leeds

Forewords

by Professor Mary Marshall, Director of Dementia Services Development Centre, Stirling University;
Mr. Rasmussen, Principal Administrator, Public Health at the European Commission

Professor Mary Marshall, Director Dementia Services Development Centre, Stirling University, Scotland:

This *CNEOPSA* Project Guide is a milestone in the emergence of a very neglected issue in dementia care: that of the care needs of people from minority groups who have dementia. The happy convergence of the European Year against Racism and Xenophobia and funds available from DG5 for work on dementia has made this important and timely project possible. I am quoted in the guide as saying that
'the world of dementia is colour blind and minority communities are dementia blind'.
This has been the case for far too long in the UK.

The danger was always going to be that the response to this state of affairs was one of stereotyped 'checklist' thinking (and there is a very useful reflection on the checklist approach in the UK section). However the authors have taken a quite different approach. In reporting on detailed and evidently sensitive interviews they shed light on the complexity of the issues. An example is the issue of communication. It is clearly too easy to say that people from minorities loose their acquired language. The reality is that speech problems resulting from dementia exacerbate communication problems in both languages. This points to the crucial importance of non-verbal communication.

In its subtle and sensitive findings this report begins to set the agenda for the further work which is urgently required both in practice and research. The author's views on awareness raising for example chime with our findings in our survey of good practice in dementia services in Europe which we undertook for the EACH (European Alzheimer Clearing House) project. Our experience was that service providers need only a small amount of encouragement and explanation to alert them to the importance of understanding the needs of local minority groups and people from minorities in their care. This guide points out that greater awareness in staff and families in contact with older people with dementia from minority groups would lead to earlier diagnosis and thereby earlier access to what help there is available.

Clearly a great deal remains to be done. This guide with its clear summary of the issues and careful reporting of very complex issues will assist all who follow on this journey to provide better dementia care to ALL our citizens.

Mr Lars Rasmussen, Principal Administrator, Public Health at the European Commission, Luxembourg:

The first international conference focusing on migration medicine was held under the auspices of the International Organisation for Migration (IOM) in Geneva in 1990. In 1992 the Commission of the European Communities and IOM jointly organised the Second International Conference on Migration and Health. Since then many national or regional meetings, workshops and conferences on migration and health have been organised.

It stands out from all these meetings that there is an outspoken need to organise specific health services for different groups or subcultures. The health systems of the Member States of the European Union are not adapted to the needs of the migrants. They are fundamentally monocultural and thus poorly equipped to meet the needs of societies that are increasingly diverse in their linguistic and cultural composition.

The absence of multicultural health services means that members of non-native ethnic groups very often experience difficulties in the interaction with health and social services designed for a different population. The cultural universe of migrants should be acknowledged. Countries like Luxembourg and Belgium with large ethnic minority groups have taken steps in this direction.

Official statistics give an idea of the dimension of the problem. In 1984 net migration of EUR 15 was close to zero. It then began to turn positive in 1985, increasing rapidly from 1988 onwards and surpassing the one million barrier in 1990. In 1992 net migration of EUR 15 was 1.2 million persons.

In order to compare, traditional receivers of migrants (USA, Canada and Australia) receive an estimated one million permanent migrants a year.

The free movement of persons, goods and services and capital will mean even larger migratory movement in the years to come, be it workers looking for jobs, older people looking for a place to retire or medical migration towards countries with more advantageous health care systems.

Migration from outside the European Union might be instrumental in alleviating the problem of the ageing of the population and the consequent fear that early in the 21st century the labour force may be insufficient to cover the needs of the elderly.

Although the numbers of the population of working age remain relatively constant (around 210 million people aged between 20 and 59) in the next ten years, there will be a shift of people aged between 20 and 29 towards people aged between 50 and 59. However during the years 2005 to 2050 a fall in the number of persons aged between 20 and 60 will be evident throughout the European Union. The lowest point will be reached around 2030.

This trend can be compensated for by a selective immigration policy. The European Commission has calculated that offsetting birth deficits on a Europe-wide basis by inward migration would mean having to increase migration to Europe from non-EU states 14-fold by the year 2025.

The Federal Republic of Germany with 7,000,000 or 9% of the population foreigners within the meaning of the country's Aliens Act occupies a top position in Europe. Where the USA had 245 immigrants for every 100,000 inhabitants on average in the years 1983 to 1988, the figures for the Federal Republic in the same period were 1,022 for every 100,000 inhabitants. In order to offset the birth deficit in Germany's Western states by immigration only net annual immigration would have to increase to 500,000 immigrants by the year 2045. Foreigners' share in the total population of the Federal Republic would amount to approximately 40%.

Such a scenario gives an indication of the actual and future size of the problem of ethnic minority groups to be tackled by national health systems.

It might perhaps even be wrong to talk of ethnic minorities but one should more appropriately talk about a multi-ethnic Europe.

Europe's population is greying. According to the second report on the demographic situation in the European Union, by 2025 the number of people aged over 60 will increase by 37 million - a growth of nearly 50% to 113.5 million pensioners in the European Union, nearly one third of the population. The migration figures from the Federal Republic of Germany show that an increasing number of these elders will belong to ethnic minority groups.

Alzheimer's disease and related disorders is associated with old age. The ageing of the population thus means a rapid increase in the number of persons suffering from this group of diseases. According to the Eurodem study 5% of those above 65 suffer from dementia of the Alzheimer type and 20% of those above 85.

Alzheimer's disease does not discriminate between sex or race, but strikes evenly. Since Alzheimer's disease is characterised by deficits in cognitive capacity, including memory, thinking, orientation, comprehension, calculation, learning capacity, language and judgement, members of ethnic minorities pose a specific challenge to the health care system in terms of diagnosis and long term care.

Diagnostic instruments are not sensitive enough to other cultural and language settings, and dementia is often diagnosed later in ethnic minorities. Patients may not speak or have the capacity to speak the language of the country where they live, making good care difficult and preventing therapies such as reminiscence and validation, leaving no other alternative but psychosomatic drugs which are often abused. Care tends to become task centred instead of person centred. Longevity is a relatively recent phenomenon and the ageing of the migrants or other ethnic minorities a relatively new issue which the health care systems will have to cope with, although 66.6 % of professionals interviewed in a study carried out by Professor Mary Marshall from the Dementia Services Development Centre in Stirling for the European Alzheimer Clearing House on "Good Practice in the Continuity of Care" showed that ethnic minority elders was not considered a problem.

The present study carried out by the *CNEOPSA* team with the support of the European Union is to my knowledge the first attempt to deal systematically with ethnic minorities and dementia.

More studies are now on their way. The Wissenschaftliche Institut der Ärzte Deutschlands (Scientific Institute of Medical Doctors in Germany) has just started a study of the prevalence and care situation of migrants with neurodegenerative diseases in the Member States of the European Union. The International Centre for Migration and Health is considering a European study on migrant family and community based responses to Alzheimer's disease.

Acknowledgements

This Guide and the work of the *CNEOPSA* Project would not have been possible without support from the European Commission, DG V, Health Promotion Unit. We are most grateful to the support and the comments provided by Mr. L. Rasmussen at the European Commission. We would also like to express our appreciation to the individual organisations in our three countries where we as authors are located and to the many individuals who gave us encouragement and support throughout the Project: these are fully expressed in the individual country acknowledgements.

At an international level, the interest and support shown by Alzheimer's Disease International, Dr. Roy (Alzheimer's & Related Disorders Society of India; organising committee of 14th ADI conference), Dr. Chandra (Centre for Ageing Research, India) and Professor Baro (EACH, Brussels) was most encouraging.

Towards the end of the project, we were delighted to receive a declaration of support from minority ethnic older people from seven European countries attending an ENAE (European Network on Ageing and Ethnicity) Euro-seminar at Maastricht. This is reproduced as Appendix 2.

This Guide is published in English, Danish and French. The final editing was done by Dr Naheed Mirza to whom we are grateful. This was done before the text was translated into Danish and French.

Finally our thanks to the publishing arrangements made in very short time by Geoffrey Mann at Russell House Publishing Ltd.

Notes on Authors

UK

Naina Patel is a Visiting Research Fellow at the Bradford Management Centre, University of Bradford, Emm Lane, Bradford BD9 4JL (Fax no:+ 44 113 295 8221). She has specialised in ageing and ethnicity in the UK, is a founding member of European Network on Ageing & Ethnicity and managed antiracist/equality in social work developments at the Central Council for Education and Training in Social Work.

Naheed R. Mirza is a Researcher at Cerebrus Ltd, Institute for Medical Research, (Oakdene Court, 613 Reading Rd, Winnersh, Wokingham RG 41 5UA). He was previously at the Institute of Psychiatry. He has specialised in clinical aspects of Alzheimer's disease and pharmocolgy.

Denmark

Peter Lindblad is a Research Fellow at the Danish Institute of Gerontology, Aurehojvej 24, 2900 Hellerup, (Fax no: +45 39 40 40 45). He specialises in ageing and ethnicity in Denmark and is a founding member of European Network on Ageing & Ethnicity.

Kirsten Amstrup is a Registered Nurse. She works at Brøndby Municipality and Danish Institute of Gerontology. She specialises in dementia care and care of the elderly.

France

Omar Samaoli is the Director of Observatoire Geontologique des Migrations (OGMF) based at Hôpital Paul Brousse, Pavillon Maurice Deparis, 94804 VILLEJUIF CEDEX, France (Fax no: +33 1 45 59 39 45). He specialises in ageing and ethnicity in France.

1. Introduction

This Guide is like a 'map' which has been designed to achieve a wider objective. But a 'map' is also a guide which directs the reader. So it is necessary at the outset to explain the purpose of this guide, the context of our work and the approach we have taken in creating this Guide. We consider the inevitable issues which emerge as a result of differences in terminology and difficulties in translations in cross-country practices.

1. The Purpose of the Guide

Ageing is not a matter of choice and consequently affects everyone irrespective of ethnicity, class, gender and disability. The fact that the number of older people from minority ethnic backgrounds is rising, is being increasingly recognised by policy makers, planners of services and professionals in all three countries selected in this the *CNEOPSA* – managing care needs for ethnic minority people suffering from Alzheimer's Disease – Project. It is a pilot-project which is supported by the European Commission (DG V). The countries considered in this project are the UK, Denmark and France. As the study and developments on the subject of ageing and ethnicity are relatively in their 'infancy' in the three countries selected, there are obvious gaps in understanding and knowledge: dementia/Alzheimer's Disease is one such area which is increasingly gaining attention as people with these diseases enter the social and health care system. Inevitably questions from ethnic minorities, some carers and professionals are being raised regarding the nature of social and health care services on offer and their delivery.

The *CNEOPSA* Project through this guide hopes to begin to make a significant contribution *within* the individual countries concerned as well as *across* Europe, by establishing the current level of progress in research, care developments, education and training in dementia/Alzheimer's disease as it concerns minority ethnic older people. It also intends to identify specific gaps in these areas and help highlight the complexities and challenges facing the field of ageing, ethnicity and management of dementia care. We consider these issues and factors in our individual country profiles. The *CNEOPSA* Project also believes that care professionals need appropriate values, knowledge and skills which are 'in tune' with the specific experiences of minority ethnic older people with Alzheimer's disease. We describe and examine the requirements professionals need in the section on country practice for each individual country.

Thus, a Good Practice Guide is a *first stage* of principles and suggestions since 'good practice' should in reality be thoroughly researched, tried and tested. However, what if the area, as in *CNEOPSA's* case, begins from a low appropriate knowledge and practice base? We could simply wait for appropriate knowledge and practice to appear or begin to highlight the appropriate research and practice work which is already taking place, and use this to develop a comprehensive plan in managing dementia care. We have chosen to pursue the latter path. The purpose of this Guide then is to:

- establish country profiles for the UK, Denmark and France;

- inform, increase awareness and improve care-taking by professional care staff;

- stimulate interest and commitment to change policy and practice among policy-makers and gerontological interests;

- produce from an informed basis, at least that which is feasible in a nine month period, a 'map' of information which helps to (i) plan future work, (ii) target developments and (iii) concentrate effort.

In short, we intended to maximise learning and practice in order to meet the aim of planning and managing quality care in dementia for minority ethnic older people. The Guide is meant as a tool for practitioners, policy-makers, planners and teachers of health and social care services concerned with the management of dementia care for minority ethnic older people. However, we recognise that the 'tool' will need further developments, new information, fresh angles, and that existing information in the Guide will have to be refined over time.

2. The Context in which CNEOPSA Project teams worked

> *"Minorities? We just had not thought of them....but now that you mention it we think it is relevant....."*

> – several respondents who provide services and training (from the EACH Project; quote summary by Professor Mary Marshall).

The quote suggests that *interest* in our subject exists, and this is encouraging. However, the quote implies that a void exists in this area – this is why we reasoned that individual country profiles had to be established.

We recognise that the *context* of working with minorities is not always seen as an area of concern in our three countries. And if it is, the issue often has to be handled with sensitivity normally accompanied by other humble attributes so as not to 'upset the sensitivities of others'. For example, it would be hard to believe that the realities of discrimination and disadvantage faced by minorities somehow stop when a minority person interacts with a professional. Professionals come from the wider society and some may bring with them the forces of racism and xenophobia when interacting with patients. In recognition of such facts as well as wider issues, the

European Parliament declared 1997 as the *European Year Against Racism*. This declaration gives recognition and legitimacy to our area of concern.

Further complexity to the context of working with minorities is added by the *heterogeneity* of our target group: in all our three countries, minority older people with dementia come from different linguistic, cultural and faith backgrounds. Furthermore, differences in social class and background migration issues also add to the picture – *e.g.* some came as a result of colonial 'link', some as a result of contracts as 'economic migrants' and some as refugees. Not all require the same range of services. This means that when talking of culturally sensitive services, the issues are not clear-cut – if they were we would have to assume that minorities with dementia are a *homogeneous* group, which is clearly not the case.

We have also considered information already generated on minorities with dementia in the USA, Canada and Australia. From studies in the USA it is clear that there are a number of issues that need to be addressed regarding ethnic minorities with dementia. For example, whilst different prevalence rates exist between Whites, Blacks and Hispanics in the USA – with Hispanics scoring highly in terms of numbers with dementia – it is clear that tests from various sources (Diagnostic and Statistical Manual of Mental Disorders – DSM-IV of the American Psychiatric Association and the National Institute of Neurological and Communicative Diseases and Stroke and Alzheimer's disease and Related Disorders Association – NINCDS-ADRDA) used to diagnose dementia are not equally sensitive in the three groups due to differences in culture, language and background (Gurland *et al.*, 1995; Bohnstedt *et al.*, 1994; Loewenstein *et al.*, 1993). In addition research has shown that environmental and genetic factors may be important (Hendrie *et al.*, 1995; Maestre *et al.*, 1995). Particularly worrying is the lack of inclusion of ethnic minorities in existing research projects on care methods and provisions as well as medical research in dementia (Ballard *et al.*, 1994; Valle, 1994; Welsh *et al.*, 1994).

Only by fully comprehending the context in which we were working could we organise a framework which allowed us to approach the subject of managing care for minority ethnic older people with dementia/Alzheimer's disease.

3. The CNEOPSA Approach

In developing our framework for this guide, we made some *baseline assumptions:*

- The mainstream world of dementia/Alzheimer's disease is "colour - blind".

- The world of minority ethnic ageing and health is "blind" to dementia/Alzheimer's disease.

- Information on the prevalence and causes of dementia/Alzheimer's disease in minority ethnic groups is problematic.

13

- Project developments for minority ethnic groups in the field of dementia/Alzheimer's disease are *either non-existent or, if they exist, developments are sketchy and ad hoc.*

- It follows from the above then that we will start from a low level of knowledge and development base.

- There is interest and commitment by various groups in this area. It requires action to support developments.

The *CNEOPSA* Project had the benefit of a multidisciplinary team whose expertise resided in the fields of ageing and ethnicity, accompanied by a specialist on Alzheimer's Disease from a clinical and nursing perspective. We were also able to determine the general context as outlined in Appendix 1, which gives useful background information on Alzheimer's Disease. This section provides an important source of information which helps generate pertinent questions as regards where 'differences' for minorities may occur. In short it enables us at particular points to ask ethnicity-related questions. The *CNEOPSA* team has also found it necessary to highlight different perspectives within the mainstream.

4. Structure of the Guide

In the Guide each country section comprises firstly a *country profile* followed by an exploration, with analysis, of their *country practice* using a selected modality (see below) to show this. Finally, the conclusion provides a shortlist of key *recommendations* in the form of summary points which are derived from the individual country profile and practice findings.

Firstly, the 'Country Profile' seeks to establish:

(1) Who the minority ethnic older people are and their socio-economic and health profiles (depending on available country information).

(2) Specific dementia/Alzheimer's disease related information: (i) epidemiological profile, (ii) predictions for the future, (iii) comparison with other countries and (iv) prevalence among ethnic minorities.

(3) The cost of Alzheimer's disease in social and health services and comparisons with other diseases.

(4) The specific knowledge areas relating to ethnic minorities: (i) research and print information, (ii) other sources of information such as ethnic minority organisations, (iii) surveys on mental health generally and (iv) government and related organisations are also considered.

This section therefore will highlight the nature of information regarding the prevalence, care and provisions made for the minority ethnic elderly with dementia in our three countries.

Secondly, each country then explores and covers one or more of the following themes: (i) The management of care involves looking at the entire person with dementia/Alzheimer's disease; (ii) Responding to the care needs of persons with dementia requires interaction of trained personnel, professional and/or family carers, with the demented person; and (iii) Organisations in turn manage this process of Care as part of their overall capacity to design, plan and manage human and financial resources. These themes can be illustrated diagrammatically (see below for the meaning of directed arrows):

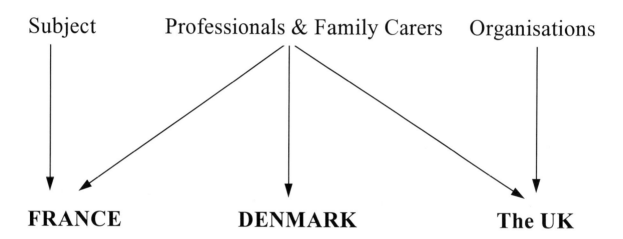

Since the country profiles confirmed our view of a low knowledge base in Europe, the purpose of this second part of the study was to generate data on some of the issues by using questionnaire, direct interview and observation methods in the UK, Denmark and France aimed at four modalities: Professionals, Organisations (general Alzheimer's disease organisations as well as those catering specifically for ethnic minorities), Carer's and the families of sufferer's. By this means we hoped to attain examples of good and bad practice, problems faced by the groups mentioned above and their recommendations and views on this area. From this data we would then make conclusions and recommendations, thus forming the basis for this Guide.

As this was a one year pilot project time precluded the generation of data from all four modalities in each of the three countries. Also, since the 'Country Profile' section highlighted similarities between the three countries regarding problems faced by minority ethnic older people with dementia it was agreed that the three countries would distribute the modalities amongst themselves. This would give more in-depth knowledge of each modality in this area, allow some cross comparisons between the countries (with the caveat that data was attained from different modalities), and play to each countries individual strengths in this area as described below. However, it is possible that differences exist in the modalities between the three countries. For this reason, other modalities were covered in a smaller way by all three countries. The arrows in the diagram above summarises each countries main focus (vertical arrows) and other modalities covered by each country in lesser detail (diagonal arrows, see below).

Denmark

In Denmark data was collected from qualitative interviews and participant observations. The qualitative interviews concentrated on the interaction between patients, their family and professionals with emphasis on the cultural and ethnic/racial context. In the interviews with GP's and geriatricians attention also focused on diagnostic issues and the problems concerning ethnicity and communication problems. The main focus in the interviews with professionals and carers was on care aspects and the interaction between the care, family and patient. Participant observations were made in a nursing home for a specific ethnic group. The observations were made by a nurse with seventeen years experience and knowledge of dementia care and was discussed and analysed with an anthropologist and academic staff at the Danish Institute of Gerontology working on dementia, ageing and ethnicity background. The Danish part concentrates on care practice. It highlights the problems facing minority ethnic older persons with dementia, and the issues affecting both the demented persons family and the care staff involved in the everyday care of the person with dementia.

France

By contrast, in France although research programmes on Alzheimer's Disease do exist – studies carried out by the INSERM laboratory and the AP-HP combined team of physicians and teachers – so far, minority ethnic older people with dementia/Alzheimer's disease have not been taken into account. Similarly the presence of minority ethnic groups have not been fully considered as a gerontological reality. So it was decided that in France questionnaires would concentrate more on the circumstances and conditions of the patient's themselves by accessing hospital and GP archives and talking to the families/carer's of the patient. Such a focus would generate a better understanding of the extent of the problem and aid in the design and delivery of care of minority ethnic older persons with dementia. Difficulties are clearly encountered in such a process of data collation. Therefore questionnaires were submitted to a range of professionals involved in the care of minorities with dementia.

United Kingdom

In the UK there are a number of general Alzheimer's disease organisations as well as a strong tradition of organisations catering for diverse minority ethnic older people. Therefore, the main questionnaire in the UK concentrates on such organisations' responses and their capacity to serve people with dementia who rely upon their services. A shorter questionnaire was also developed and aimed at professionals. Furthermore, some data from carers will also be provided to give a more comprehensive picture of the issues in the UK. The data and analysis drawn from professionals and carers is important because it allows for a direct comparison with the findings from Denmark and France, respectively.

It is anticipated that the data generated by the three countries may provide useful planning tools on the management of care for minority ethnic older persons with dementia. In addition, examination of how professionals interact with minority ethnic elders and what the key issues are for carers in the management and care of this group may lead to a better understanding of how the system of care relates to minority ethnic older people with dementia.

We chose not to take a short-cut view of this area by relying upon our previous experience and materials to generate conclusions and recommendations. Instead, as outlined above, we focused on different modalities in the three countries so that the conclusions and recommendations we generated were from an informed basis. This is important because not everyone involved in the care of minority ethnic older people with dementia believe that it merits particular attention. We therefore hope that this Guide will help achieve the aims expressed above under the heading 'The purpose of the Guide'.

5. Terminology and Translation

There are differences in usage of certain terms in each of the three countries which may carry a different meaning for the reader. These include:

(i)   Migrants, minorities, ethnic minority, minority ethnic, black people – as a result of internal European migration, colonial background or refugee status. The terms are all used to a varying degree by the three countries. We have therefore tried not to come up with one single term applicable to the three countries. This is because we may end up losing the focus of the issues at hand by debating whether a selected term is appropriate or not in each country.

(ii)   Carers – in Denmark this refers to professional carers while in the UK this term can be used for both family and professional carers.

(iii) Residential care is an accepted term in the UK while in France the shorthand is not used.

6. Authors' views and responsibilities

This Guide comprises a common introduction (above) and conclusion – the views expressed within which are shared by all authors of this Guide.

However, for individual countries, authors were responsible for developing their respective modality and producing their country scripts. The respective authors' views for the Country Profile and Practice are therefore their own.

United Kingdom

Naina Patel and Naheed R. Mirza

Acknowledgements

Our work was a large collaborative effort. In addition to those mentioned in the Introduction of the Guide, our thanks to Professors Weir and Sparkes for supporting the *CNEOPSA* project at the Bradford Management Centre. They were both generous with their time and a source of encouragement. Liz Wulff-Cochrane and Mick Farrant at the Central Council for Education and Training in Social Work made it possible for one of us to be seconded to the Project: our thanks for their personal support and interest. Professor Marshall (Stirling University), Professor Sashidharan (Birmingham University), Tom Kitwood (Bradford University), Dr. Rafiq Gardee (Multicultural Health Glasgow), Mr. Balmukund Pareekh (Gita Foundation), Jenny Bourne (Institute of Race Relations) Suzanne Munday (VOCAL, Edinburgh) and our respective family members all played a large part in stimulating us with ideas and occasional critique while supporting the direction of our work.

We would like to extend our warm thanks to colleagues at Alzheimer's Disease Society and in particular Clive Evers who made suggestions on the first draft. We appreciated the comments to our first draft from Social Services Inspectors, Department of Health in particular Reba Bhaduri, Derek Brown and Raymond Warburton.

Our sincere thanks and appreciation to all the individuals and organisations who took part in our survey. They gave their time inspite of huge workload pressures and genuinely wanted us to convey the state of current situation to help improve dementia care to minority ethnic older people in the UK

Beulah Mills, Rashida Pocketawala, Sally Davies, Rosalie André, Ricky Tang, and Jill Bochel all played a large part in contributing directly or indirectly to interviews and data collation: we appreciated their intense effort and sense of care.

Our special thanks to Sue Hillas (secretarial support) and Axélle Giroud and various colleagues at the Management Centre who contributed to the Project – and to the many individuals who enquired about our work and in turn encouraged us of the importance of completing such a task. Our thanks also to *CNEOPSA* partners, Peter Lindblad and Omar Samaoli. This was afterall a large enterprise.

Part 1: The UK Country Profile

1. The General Context of minority ethnic elderly

In the UK in the late 1990's there is an increasing awareness amongst black and minority ethnic older people of their status, and they are making greater demands for improved rights and services. The ageing of black and minority ethnic people has also been recognised by public institutions, as reflected in the emergence of policy and practice – *i.e.* project developments and research. A decade earlier, several locally based empirical studies examined the needs and demands of black and minority ethnic elderly, but several areas of gerontology remained unexplored: for example, research into specific health provision issues is still in its infancy. Among these are various aspects of dementia/Alzheimer's disease. As explained in the introduction it is the intention of the *CNEOPSA* Project to determine the current status of research, development and training in the area of dementia care relating to black and minority ethnic older people. This will help determine the path for progress in the future.

Therefore, in Part 1 we establish the UK profile by first considering who the black and minority ethnic older people are and their socio-economic and health status. We then show the epidemiological profile, understanding, research interests and cost of dementia in the UK, specifically relating to minority ethnic older people. In Part 2, we first present our results and analysis of data generated from interviewing various organisations, professionals and carers (Section 1: UK practice and managing care – Key Elements). From this we suggest recommendations and solutions for the welfare of minority ethnic older persons with dementia (Section 2: The Management of Care).

The demographic facts

Everyone has ethnicity and an ethnic identity. The term 'ethnic minorities', 'minority ethnic groups', 'black people' *etc.* all generate some discussion and disagreement. For our purposes we will use the broad terms 'black' and 'minority ethnic people', and use the shorthand terms 'minority ethnic' or 'minorities' in the text to signify the fact that *"they are both relatively small in number and are in some way oppressed or subjected to inferior treatment on account of their ethnic or racial identity"* (Giddens, 1993, cited in Ratcliffe 1996, pg. 4). We will also recognise that this broad terminology, divided into ten sub-categories for census collection in 1991, *"conflates an enormous number of groups with quite distinct cultural, spatial and religious heritage's; for example, a variety of northern European groups, including the indigenous British and, significantly, the Irish and those of Greek or Turkish origin (including Cypriots of both national origins)"* (Ratcliffe, 1996 pg. 5). Similar issues arise with other sub-categories but they provide useful statistical information and are a marked improvement on previous census' as these used 'country of birth' to determine ethnicity giving an inaccurate picture of minority ethnic groups since many were (are) born in the UK. The 1991 Census for the first time determined ethnicity without resorting to 'country of birth', but it specifically omitted the category 'Irish' amid demands. Owen (1996) provides a good discussion on various aspects of ethnic classification and its under-enumeration. It should be noted that although we are speaking of Great Britain when considering ethnicity in the census figures, in N. Ireland (a part of the UK) the census did not include the 'ethnic question' despite its sizeable minority population in the country and a strong case having been put forward by minority ethnic groups for its inclusion.

A black and minority ethnic presence in the UK has not been a recent phenomenon – with the Irish in the 16th, 17th and 18th centuries and the Jews, the Poles and other minority groups in the late 19th and 20th century – the migration of people from the Caribbean and Indian sub-continent mainly dates from the post-war period. According to the 1991 Census there were some 3.2 million minority ethnic people constituting some 5.5% of the total population in the Great Britain. Their presence extends to most districts of Great Britain and N. Ireland, making the UK a multi-ethnic society.

Table 1 below shows the distribution of the population in Great Britain according to age and ethnicity. It shows the relative youth of the minority ethnic population compared to the White population and the diversity in patterns of ageing amongst different ethnic groups. Nevertheless, over 3 percent of minority ethnic people are in the over 65 years of age category compared to 16 percent of the White population. That is, of some total 8.8 million people aged 65+ years, 97,000 were from minority ethnic groups. In the 85+ age group, minority ethnic groups account for 3,871 people from a total population of 830,678. If we consider the share that minority ethnic and White groups make of the total population in different age ranges, we find that minority ethnic groups make up 1.3 and 4 percent of the 65+ and 45-64 year age ranges, respectively, compared to 98.7 and 96 percent for the corresponding age ranges for White groups (Owen, 1996; Warnes, 1996). This means that during the next decade there will be an increased percentage of minority ethnic people reaching retirement age hence changing the above profile. Moreover, there are variations in the ageing profile in minority ethnic groups depending upon location and gender, with *"females more numerous but the sex ratio of 1.006 % was slight in comparison to the ratio of 1.069 in the White population"* (Warnes, 1996, pg. 161).

Table 1: Age breakdown of ethnic groups in Great Britain, 1991
(Note: based on data adjusted for Census underenumeration)

Ethnic Group	Total population	Percentage of total population					
		Age 0-4	Age 5-15	Age 16-24	Age 25-44	Age 45-64	Age 65+
White	52,893.9	6.5	13.0	12.9	29.3	19.2	19.3
Ethnic minority groups	3,117.0	11.1	21.7	16.4	32.9	13.6	4.2
Black	*925,5*	*11.1*	*18.0*	*16.5*	*33.8*	*15.4*	*5.1*
— Caribbean	517.1	7.6	14.1	15.3	33.4	21.8	7.7
— African	221.9	11.8	17.1	17.0	42.7	9.5	1.8
— Other	186.4	20.1	29.6	19.3	24.6	4.4	1.6
South Asian	*1,524.3*	*10.9*	*24.6*	*16.5*	*30.5*	*13.5*	*3.9*
— Indian	865.5	8.9	20.5	15.5	34.9	14.9	5.2
— Pakistani	491.0	13.2	29.2	17.9	26.1	11.3	2.4
— Bangladeshi	167.8	15.1	31.9	17.9	20.8	12.7	1.5
Chinese and other	*667.2*	*11.6*	*20.1*	*16.1*	*36.9*	*11.4*	*3.8*
— Chinese	162.4	7.1	16.0	18.4	41.4	12.7	4.4
— Other - Asians	204.3	8.0	16.2	15.1	43.6	13.7	3.1
— Other - Other	300.5	16.4	25.0	15.5	29.9	9.2	3.9
Entire population	55,969.2	6.7	13.5	13.1	29.5	18.9	18.5

Source: Owen, D. (1996) pg. 116

The socio-economic position and research studies

The diversity in age distribution, location concentrations – some 45% of all minority ethnic groups reside in Greater London (Owen, 1996) – and gender differences, reflect the pattern of migration and settlement. This process has also determined the social and economic position of today's minority ethnic elders. Their social and health care needs cannot be understood without reference to their experience of employment, housing and income.

The early surveys from the Policy Studies Institute (1977; 1984) explained the unequal distribution of minority ethnic workers in the 70's (*i.e.* the elders of today) by sector and industry, as being due to differences in labour requirements between various industries and discrimination by employers and unions.   Once in jobs, discrimination in earnings followed suit. The disparity in earnings as regards 'working period' as well as the length of working life, coupled with known under-claiming of welfare benefits, account for differences in pensionable income (Askham *et al.,* 1995). For the emerging generation of elders we must add the effects of long-term unemployment, characterised by the decline of the manufacturing base (foundries, textiles, transport) where many ethnic minorities had been concentrated. These factors may contribute to the use of services in many centres by minority ethnic elders beginning from the age of 55 years. This has serious implications for policy since there may be 'early ageing' amongst this group.

Minority ethnic elders face a range of health problems, and mainstream health and social services have been inadequate in meeting their needs (Bhalla & Blakemore, 1981; Farrah, 1986; Patel 1990; Pharoah, 1995; Askham *et al.,* 1995; Lindesay *et al.,* 1997). Table 2 (a – d) shows a range of health problems that ethnic minority elders suffer from compared to the indigenous White population or Europeans, as well as evidence for a relatively higher frequency of using health services, including general practitioners (GP's), by elderly Afro-Caribbean and Asians compared to White groups. However, frequency of contact with GP's and hospitals does not necessarily reflect the quality of treatment received (Table 2c).

Table 2a: Prevalence of diagnosis in Asian and indigenous subjects

(percent)

	Asian		Indigenous	
	Men	*Women*	*Men*	*Women*
	(n = 34)	*(n = 25)*	*(n = 34)*	*(n = 25)*
Myocardial infarction	21	0	9	0
Diabetes mellitus	6	16	9	0
Hypertension	12	16	24	16
Stroke	9	4	3	0
Chronic bronchitis	3	8	18*	12
Asthma	9	12	0	4
Peptic ulcer	6	12	0	8

Note: * $p < 0.05$ (Asian men versus indigenous men).
Source: Ebrahim *et al* (1991:59)

Table 2b: Common problems of old age in Asian and indigenous subjects

	Asian		Indigenous	
	Men	*Women*	*Men*	*Women*
	(n = 34)	*(n = 25)*	*(n = 34)*	*(n = 25)*
Visual impairment	15	8	15	4
Hearing impairment	35	24	26	20
Depressed mood	6	8	0	16
Low life satisfaction	53	64	79	80*
Falls	6	16	18	24
Incontinence of urine	3	8	9	12
Use of walking stick	25	8	6	4*
On prescribed medication	68	72	41	40**

Notes: * p<0.05 (Asian men versus indigenous men).
** p<0.05 (Both groups).
Source: Ebrahim *et al* (1991:59)

Table 2c: Contact with GP and hospital (per cent)

Contact	Afro-Caribbean	Asians	Europeans
Seen GP within last month	68	57	57
Visited hospital because of ill health in past 12 months	42	25	29
Been an inpatient in hospital in past 12 months	20	13	15

Source: Bhalla and Blakemore (1981:26)

Table 2d(i): The level of knowledge and potential use of services (per cent)

	Service Unknown		Potential use	
Service	*Asian*	*White*	*Asian*	*White*
District nurse	57	14	80	78
Bath nurse	76	32	66	69
Chiropody	64	9	75	82
Home help	62	1	54	78
Meals on wheels	58	0	54	62
Social workers	44	6	69	74
Day care	60	18	54	59
(N)	(81)	(55)		

Note: Author's modification in title. Table excludes those who already receive services, so *N* varies by service. *Source*: Atkin *et al* (1989:441)

Table 2d(ii): The level of knowledge and potential use of services (per cent)

Contact**	Asian		Indigenous	
	Men	*Women*	*Men*	*Women*
	(n = 34)	*(n = 25)*	*(n = 34)*	*(n = 25)*
Seen GP within last month	26	44	24	24
Visited hospital because of ill health in past 12 months	41	52	41	48
Been an inpatient in hospital in past 12 months	24	12	6	4*
Seen nurse within last month	0	8	6	0
Seen chiropodist within last 6 months	3	4	6	24*
	44	32	56	60*
Seen dentist within last year	65	56	59	68
Seen optician within last year	3	20	0	8
Seen alternative practitioner within last year	24	12	6	4*
Hospital inpatient				

Notes: * p<0.05 (Asian women versus indigenous women).

** *Author's adaptation of categories*

Source: Ebrahim *et al* (1991:60)

Taking the studies cited above between 1981 and 1997, the findings conclusively show:

- lack of knowledge/information not only on services but also on financial entitlements;

- low take-up of residential care;

- low take-up on day care;

- low take-up on home care.

These studies also indicate that there is a demand for the use of the services noted above, with a qualification: that these services must appropriately reflect minority ethnic peoples' beliefs and practices - in other words, be appropriate, adequate and accessible. For example, recent studies by Askham (1995) and Boneham *et al.* (1997) have reinforced the idea that language barriers need to be removed and staff from the same cultural background as the person being cared for, need to be employed. Although the studies cited mainly focus on Afro-Caribbean, Asian and Chinese older people, similar inferences can be made for other minority ethnic groups on the basis of their minority status and cultural difference from the majority population. For example, Bowling and Farquhar (1993) make similar observations on the appropriateness of services and the role played by the Jewish Welfare Board in the East End of London for Jewish older people. Hickman and Walter (1997) have recently catalogued experiences of discrimination faced by the Irish community: since this includes older Irish people some extrapolations and observations can be made regarding the discrimination faced by the elderly from these communities. However, this is not to suggest that such studies can replace specific community based studies of minority ethnic older peoples' health and care requirements. Indeed much specific community work needs to be done both in the building of knowledge as well as project innovations. It is only when this occurs that we can begin to 'map out' the common trends and discern differences in relation to dementia care of older people from different minority ethnic background.

Effects of Legislation

The difficulties that minority ethnic elders face are further exacerbated within the current context of reduced welfare services and the implementation of the NHS and Community Care Act which introduced the mixed market of care. For example, we know that inner cities and poverty accompany one another. Inner cities are characterised by poor housing and previous low availability of health resources. According to the 1991 Census, minorities are concentrated in key centres and in inner city conurbation's. With a reduction and restructuring of welfare resources, any withdrawal of health resources from inner cities would have an adverse effect on the minority ethnic elderly and compound their problems in accessing services. This is all the more worrying when you consider the marked absence of minority ethnic elderly's health issues in the many splendid documents produced by the Department of Health (1993 – 1997), and supported by the Ethnic Health Unit (now closed), as a result of the government's nation of health targets (White paper, 1992). If the absence of minority ethnic elderly issues as a general category is anything to go by, then our work highlights the level of urgency required in the field of ageing, ethnicity and dementia. Moreover, it also suggests that further work is necessary to examine how the Carers Act 1996, government initiatives such as the Patient's Charter – Mental Health Services 1997, and the Care Programme Approach for People with Mental Illness have responded to the care issues of minority ethnic older people with dementia.

2. Dementia/Alzheimer's disease in the UK

This section describes the epidemiological profile and establishes the current developments in research, information and projects in the UK to provide us with the current country profile.

Epidemiological profile

Prevalence according to age

By the year 2001 fifteen percent of the UK population will be over 65 – representing over one in six people. Since Alzheimer's disease increases in frequency as we get older it will become a greater concern for society in general. Table 3 shows its prevalence in different age groups in the UK (OPCS, 1989; 1994 in Barnes, 1997).

Table 3: Prevalence of dementia in the UK

Age (years)	Prevalence by age
40-65	1.0% (1 in 100)
65-70	2.0% (1 in 50)
70-80	5.0% (1 in 20)
80 plus	20.0% (1 in 5)

Predictions for the future

In 1992 it was estimated that over 0.5 million people over the age of 40 suffered from Alzheimer's disease. It is predicted that by the year 2021 approximately 0.75 million people over the age of 40 will have Alzheimer's disease – *i.e.* 42 new cases of Alzheimer's disease every day for the next ten years. Table 4 below shows this rise (OPCS, 1989; Barnes, 1997).

Table 4: Predictions for the prevalence of dementia

Year	Prevalence of AD in the 40+ age group
1991	598,550
2001	659,997
2011	703,917
2021	900,000

There are numerous studies on the prevalence of Alzheimer's disease and it is generally quoted from integrative analysis of many of these studies that the prevalence of dementia roughly doubles every five years after the age of 60. This was shown to be the case across Europe in a re-analysis of six European studies under the auspices of EURODEM, a European union concerted action (Rocca *et al.*, 1991). The same pattern emerges for the UK from a study by Paykel *et al.* (1994) in Cambridge who used the Mini-Mental State Examination (MMSE), a commonly used assessment scale for dementia, followed by the Cambridge Examination for Mental Disorders of the Elderly (CAMDEX) interview to assess dementia. In a sample of 1,195 elderly subjects aged 75+ they found an incidence of Alzheimer's disease of 2.3 percent (aged 75-79), 4.6 percent (aged 80-84) and 8.5 percent (85-89), respectively.

Comparison with other countries

Using accepted diagnostic criteria for Alzheimer's disease – Diagnostic and Statistical Manual of Mental Disorders (DSM IV) and the National Institute of Neurological and Communicative Diseases and Stroke and Alzheimer's disease and Related Disorders Association (NINCDS/ADRDA) workgroup – recent population studies suggest that the UK may be facing a worse problem than some of its European neighbours[1] (Table 5 - taken from Rocca *et al.*, 1991).

Prevalence amongst ethnic minorities

Information on the prevalence of Alzheimer's disease in ethnic minorities is scant and research suggests that it is a 'hidden problem' as opposed to 'non-existent' (Brownlie, 1991). However, some estimate can be made. Figures from the 1991 census showed that there were 97,100 people from ethnic minority groups in Britain of 65 years and over. If we assume a similar ratio of one in 20 as for the general population (see Table 3), then there are an estimated 5,000 people from ethnic minorities with Alzheimer's disease in the UK[1] (from Alzheimer's Disease Association, UK; Owen, 1996; see also Barnes, 1997).

---

[1] In Table 5 the population sample in the UK study was aged 75+ and as stated above, every 5 years beyond the age of 60 the prevalence of Alzheimer's disease doubles - this may account for the apparent higher prevalence rate in the UK.

Table 5: Selected recent prevalence studies of Alzheimer's disease in Europe and the United States

Site	Authors	Sample	Annual Prevalence (%)
Europe			
Finland (All)	Sulkava *et al.*, 1985	1880 aged 65+	3.4
Sweden (Lundby)	Rorsman *et al.*, 1986	3563 aged 60+	2.2
Italy (Appignano)	Rocca *et al.*, 1990	550 aged 65+	3.3
UK (Cambridge)	O'Conner *et al.*, 1989	2311 aged 75+	7.9
United States			
Southern California	Pfeffer *et al.*, 1987	817 aged 65+	6.2
Minnesota (Rochester)	Kokmen *et al.*, 1975	5900 aged 65+	3.5
Maryland (Baltimore)	Folstein *et al.*, 1991	923 aged 65+	2.0

The Cost of Alzheimer's disease in the UK

Health and Social Services costs

If the cost of Alzheimer's disease to health and social services in the UK is studied it can be broken down into a number of component parts which reflect the different types of services available – this includes in- and out- patient care at mental and acute/geriatric hospitals, different forms of residential care available (private, voluntary and local authority), day care centres, general practice consultations *etc.* The major finding is that the total cost of Alzheimer's disease to the health and social services was £1144 M in 1992 and that the 75+ age group accounted for 94% of these costs. Also of note was that most of the expenditure was for institutional care rather than care in the community, emphasizing the burden on the health and social systems in the UK (Gray and Fenn, 1994).

Cost of Alzheimer's Disease in comparison to other diseases

Although when compared to other major diseases such as stroke, heart disease, diabetes and arthritis, Alzheimer's disease is a middle ranking disease in terms of costs to the health services – *e.g.* £350 M compared to £838 M for stroke – this does not take into account the social care costs associated with Alzheimer's disease. When both health and social costs are combined Alzheimer's disease is a major cost to the country – £1373 M compared to £838 M (stroke) and £668 M (heart disease), for example (1992 figures, taken from Gray and Fenn, 1994).

Research and Print Information

In the UK little research on the issue of dementia/Alzheimer's disease and ethnicity has been done. However, we have been able to ascertain some of the major groups in the UK who are addressing this issue:

- Dr Marcus Richards at the University of London, initially funded by the Alzheimer's Disease Society (ADS), has been doing a pilot project comparing a small group of White and Afro-Caribbean elderly people on various aspects of health, including mental illness and dementia. The sample included 45 people from each group over the age of 65, from South Peckham in London. The study included cognitive tests, a medical examination and an interview about background and medical history to ascertain any possible exposure to factors known to increase the risk of Alzheimer's disease. The main finding was that elderly Afro-Caribbeans had larger family networks, were more likely to have someone at home with them and were more impaired in activities of daily living than Whites. However, despite these differences in family structures there was no evidence that elderly Afro-Caribbeans were helped or supported by their families anymore than elderly Whites: "*This may be important since it is widely assumed that the health needs of the ethnic minorities in the UK are adequately met by supportive family networks*" (Richards, 1996 in ADS newsletter).

- Professor James Lindesay and colleagues at Leicester have evaluated a Gujarati version of the MMSE by comparing its sensitivity as a screening instrument for dementia amongst Gujarati speaking older people and British-born Whites (Lindesay, 1997, forthcoming). The study found that the Gujarati version of the MMSE "*performed comparably in both groups as a screen for moderate-severe dementia, but was less efficient at detecting milder and less certain cases in the Gujarati group*". The estimated prevalence of confirmed dementia was higher in the Gujarati group, but this was not statistically significant. Since this was a pilot study, the authors rightly suggest that the Gujarati version of the MMSE needs to be further evaluated in a larger sample group, as well as in clinical samples and native Indian Gujaratis.

- Dr Alistair Burns' group at Manchester University have an ongoing project in which they are assessing Instruments used in Alzheimer's disease research and diagnosis, to ascertain their sensitivity to Alzheimer's disease in different ethnic groups. This work is being carried out by Dr. Greta Rait. This is important because one of the major issues that arises from research in the US is that ethnic groups may be under or over represented as suffering from Alzheimer's disease due to an insensitivity of the Instruments used. In particular there is a high prevalence of Hispanics with Alzheimer's disease compared to Blacks and Whites in some studies, and this is thought to stem from an insensitivity of the Instruments used and the level of training the clinician has regarding language and cultural differences (Bohnstedt *et al.*, 1994).

- Dr. Margaret Boneham and colleagues at Liverpool University are involved in a two-phase Health and Ethnicity Project in the city, that is now in its second phase. They have identified approximately 71 minority ethnic older people living in Liverpool's inner city as suffering from dementia and/or depression. The project has essentially looked at the characteristics of the respondents, barriers to services they have encountered and the level of unmet need. The group used the lack of knowledge and lack of intent barriers typology of Yeatts *et al.* (cited in Boneham et al. 1997). They conclude that there is a need to increase medical services to the target group and that further work should be done in conjunction with minority ethnic groups.

- Professor Mary Marshall is the Director of the Dementia Study Group at Stirling University in Scotland. A study by Brownlie (1991) from this group emphasizes the lack of information on this subject and draws on research on ethnicity more generally, concluding that Alzheimer's disease in ethnic groups is a hidden problem that needs to be addressed. The group holds an extensive database on Alzheimer's disease and ethnicity. However, when perusing this database it is notable that many of the UK based studies are general with few specifically addressing the issue of ethnicity and Alzheimer's disease.

- Other databases. A search of a database on CD-ROM from the Centre for Policy on Ageing was also used to ascertain whether there was any print information in this area. Again there was general information on ageing. Searches using keywords such as ethnic, minority and cultural in combination with Alzheimer's, dementia or ageing gave no relevant information. Using the keywords Polish, African, Caribbean, Asian, Italian and Jewish gave more references but nothing specifically relating to Alzheimer's disease in these groups. An extensive Medline search was also done but much of the information was general. Any information on the issue of ethnicity and Alzheimer's disease was predominantly from the US.

- The Alzheimer's Disease Society and in particular its Director of Information and their officer with an ethnic minorities brief, Helen Sawyer, in its London branch, have been helpful in assisting with relevant information. There is also an ethnic minority specialist appointed, Alaba Okuyiga, in the Birmingham ADS office who is pursuing targeted areas of development for its minority ethnic groups. The ADS newsletter which gives Reviews and Comment on the Epidemiology, Pathogenesis and Management of Alzheimer's disease is particularly useful for keeping in touch with treatments provided by smaller groups in nursing homes *etc.*, which may be appropriate for the mainstream and ethnic minorities. The Society also supported Dr. Richard's research cited above.

- The Social Services Inspectorate (SSI), Department of Health (DH), led by Derek Brown's team have recently undertaken a National Inspection of Services for Older People with Dementia. This provides very useful information highlighting best practice and *general* themes which indicate a "standard" for equality of opportunity. As for the data, out of a sample of 382 cases, six clients with dementia were identified as belonging to a "visible minority" group, plus two more who spoke French and German, respectively. Regrettably our request to interview these minorities could not be accommodated due to difficulties in tracing the individuals.

- In the same series as that above, although not an Inspection Study, the SSI report 'Older people with mental health problems living alone: anybody's priority?' (1997), which was compiled on the basis of visits to four local authorities and workshops, makes some observations on minority ethnic groups. It concurs with our view that minority ethnic older people with dementia are a neglected group: "*The majority of social care services for older people can be criticised for not being culturally sensitive to the needs of black elders, and there is a tendency to assume that black people belong to a homogeneous group and will wish to use whatever special services are provided.....Being unable to campaign for the services which they would like, it is all too often concluded that black elders are not in need of services. However the number of older mentally ill people in the minority ethnic communities is increasing, and planning must not be influenced by the current low uptake of services*" (pg. 33).

- The National Institute of Social Work led by Joe Moriarty has just completed research on how care is delivered by professional staff. Out of 206 people in the survey, only two emerged from a minority ethnic background.

Other Sources

We referred to our own knowledge of relevant organisations as well as the Health Education Authority's (HEA) directories on organisations involved in mental health issues in the UK. There are two categories – organisations providing help and information for different ethnic groups and those catering for demented elderly people generally. Some of these groups have been contacted and some comment on their activities is given below. Others will be contacted in the future. Of those contacted thus far, the overall conclusion is that there is little knowledge regarding Alzheimer's disease in ethnic minorities.

(i) Black and ethnic minority organisations

- The Advocacy project are based in Liverpool and are a community based service supporting and encouraging ethnic minorities to challenge inappropriate procedures, practices and treatments within the mental health system. However, almost all their referrals are schizophrenics with, surprisingly, hardly any referrals with other mental illnesses. They had no print information on the main issues relating to the problems minorities had in accessing and dealing with the health system.

- The Mental Health Shop is based in Leicester and has information on mental health issues concerning ethnic minorities. Most of this is aimed at the Asian and Afro-Caribbean communities and is in the form of leaflets and brochures.

- Standing conference of ethnic minority senior citizens (SCEMSC). This is an umbrella organisation which aims to be a resource and reference centre for any person or organisation seeking advice to instigate research on elderly Asian and ethnic minority peoples.

- Over 20 minority based organisations covering different ethnic groups and scope of area (i.e. community work from mental health to ageing) were contacted. Considering this low information base on Alzheimer's disease in the UK, our project and known work on ageing and ethnicity, invitations to meet and speak at events have been rising – this is particularly poignant within the context of the European Year Against Racism.

(ii) White and majority organisations specialising in Dementia, Alzheimer's disease and Ageing

- Alzheimer Scotland are based in Edinburgh and promote a campaign entitled 'Action on Dementia'. They have produced a number of leaflets such as "What is dementia?" and "Getting help" in various community languages. However, when asked why they had these leaflets and what the perceived reasons were, they had no real basis for producing them. Nevertheless, the issue of developing tapes – audio or video – as a better means of communicating dementia issues to ethnic minorities was discussed, particularly considering that many first generation people of ethnic minority backgrounds cannot read or write in their spoken language.

- Alzheimer's Disease Society (England) – reference is already made in (i) above. In addition, regional centres in three areas had undertaken awareness raising exercises among minorities, including translation of leaflets. Meetings will continue with key officers.

- Alzheimer's Concern in Ealing with its ethnic minority officer Kulbir Gill, has developed work to raise awareness among minority groups and is currently undertaking research on Asian women and depression – an issue of concern since depression is often confused with dementia/Alzheimer's disease. This group also run Penny Sangam, a weekend respite care centre for its local multi-racial population. It is managed by Mr. Sandu and his multi-racial and multi-professional team.

Several other organisations catering for older people were contacted, but most had no print information on Alzheimer's disease among minority ethnic older people.

(iii) Reminiscence Work

Importantly, some minority ethnic organisations have developed and used a reminiscence approach. We noted for example that the Ekta Project (Neighbour-hood Care Project) in London led by Ramesh Verma produce Reminiscence play *Hamari Kahani* performed by the Project's elderly members and volunteers. Similarly with professional actors the Age Exchange Reminiscence Theatre, under the aegis of Pam Schweitzer, has produced a play *Roots* about the experiences of migration. The idea of designating a room to Reminiscence work within a Day Centre at WISE in Brent (London) is the creation of its Co-ordinator, Mr. Filson. The Room is well used and valued by its members.

Surveys on mental health and other general information

- *Health* Education Authority – This organisation had no information on ethnic issues in dementia specifically and they currently do not see it as a target issue.

- NHS Ethnic Health Unit Directory/DH Resource Directory – No references to projects or materials could be found on dementia/Alzheimer's disease.

Indirect contacts – Some of this is incorporated in the sections above.

- Although the Bradford Dementia Group led by Dr. Tom Kitwood have not done any work in the area of minorities and Alzheimer's disease, their general approach and Dementia Care Planning may highlight developments in the mainstream that can be considered for its transferability to the care of minorities.

3. Conclusion

- The general epidemiological trends in the UK appear to be similar to those in other industrialized nations – namely an anticipated dramatic increase in the prevalence of Alzheimer's disease over the next 30 years or so, which current health systems would not be able to cope with. As regards minority ethnic older people there are no studies specifically looking at the prevalence of Alzheimer's disease in these populations. Furthermore, preliminary data from Marcus Richards' group at the University of London suggests that the prevailing dogma that minorities are aided by the extended family and therefore require less help from the social and health services appears to be false. However this finding has been known to us for over a decade and shows that those from the field of dementia who are new to ethnicity have as much to learn as we do about the field of dementia.

- Although, there are a number of people, groups and organisations doing research, much of this is in its infancy and real hard data is difficult to access (even from the Burns group in Manchester who are two years into their project). The scarcity of the number of projects and the fact that the one's that do exist are in their infancy suggests that this area is only now being given some recognition. This is recognised by some experts in this area: Marshall (1997) in her edited collection of 44 contributions in 'state of the art in dementia care', comments on the *"omission of any specific contribution on dementia care and minority ethnic groups....it is an issue, with few exceptions, neglected by British contributors. This issue deserves urgent attention. There is a major gap in British literature as a whole"*(pg. xiv and xv).

- Government initiatives on mental health, including dementia, give recognition to minority ethnic older peoples' needs in terms of access and appropriateness of services. The specific statements made in the Social Services Inspectorate reports which we have cited are also encouraging. This encouragement, however, is to no avail if there are no *specifically designated initiatives* designed to stimulate developments so as to provide appropriate dementia care in practice.

From the above it is apparent that there are a number of organisations, bodies and groups interested in the area of dementia and minority ethnic groups but none of these appears to have much information that is readily available. What we are having to do is to trace the small base of information from various locations, as well as help to generate information from the field– characteristic of the area of ethnicity.

Part 2: UK Practice And Managing Care – Key Elements

SECTION 1: Establishing the nature of Practice

Introduction

Although in the UK there are a number of general Alzheimer's Disease organisations, there is also a strong tradition of organisations catering for different ethnic minority groups in the country. There are now several minority ethnic organisations catering for the day care or residential needs of minority ethnic older people. These organisations have emerged with or without the support of mainstream organisations and provide a range of services (Norman 1985; Patel, 1990; Blakemore and Boneham, 1994; Askham *et al.*, 1995). Within the context of a mixed economy, structured welfare and the implementation of the NHS and Community Care Act in 1993, the existence of black and minority ethnic elderly organisations as the providers of services is critical.

If the management of care needs of minorities with dementia is to be properly addressed from the point of view of policy and the capacity of organisations to plan and provide care, then our examination of this area must begin with the critical players. Therefore, our main questionnaire concentrated on minority ethnic organisations catering for the elderly. A shorter questionnaire was also developed and aimed at professionals working with minority ethnic older people suffering from dementia. Furthermore, some data relating to family carers was also generated so as to give a more complete picture. The data from professionals and carers was important because it allowed for a comparison with the findings in Denmark and France, respectively.

It is anticipated that the data generated by these questionnaires may provide useful planning tools for the management of care of with dementia. In addition, how professionals interact with minority ethnic elderly and what the key issues are for carers in the management and care of this group, may lead to a better understanding of how the *system of care* relates to minority ethnic older people with dementia.

Methodology

General Approach

The interviews were conducted with minority ethnic residential or day care organisations (with specific questions on carers, which are supplemented with two case studies – see below), and professionals located in England and Scotland. All interviews were conducted between June and September 1997. When contacted, organisations and professionals were given some background information on the *CNEOPSA* Project and its aims, either verbally (telephone or face-to-face) or *via* literature (post). Professionals were initially screened to determine whether or not they had had contact with minority ethnic elderly with dementia. After agreeing to and having been interviewed professionals were asked if they had knowledge of others who would be interested in this project and in answering our questions – thus creating a 'snowball' effect.

Details on the two questionnaires is given below. However, due to the pilot nature of the project both questionnaires were designed so as to give plenty of scope for individual comments and views to ascertain whether common themes and ideas recurred other than those listed in the questionnaires themselves. Interviewees were also asked whether or not they could be quoted directly from the completed forms.

Organisations

There were 12 organisations interviewed using the questionnaires, all of which catered for ethnic minority older people. Ten of these interviews were conducted face-to-face with managers and a visit to the organisation itself to establish a rapport, whereas two were conducted via the telephone. There were a number of criteria and considerations in choosing the organisations for this study:

- Ethnicity spread – to cover a number of different ethnic minority groups, including Afro-Caribbean, Chinese, Polish, Asian and Jewish.

- Geography – organisations from selected cities of England and Scotland were chosen to reflect the demographic spread of ethnic minorities in these countries.

- A cross-section of day centres and residential homes were questioned.

- The criteria that all organisations should have contact with minority ethnic elderly with dementia and that they were managing some form of care was crucial.

The questionnaire itself consisted of 34 questions that could be grouped into three broad categories relating to specific issues:

- *Background on organisation* – who the main service users were and the services provided by the organisation.

- *Dementia* – where the organisations referral's had come from, diagnostic issues and issues on the care provided.

- *Ethnicity and Dementia* – views on barriers facing minority ethnic elderly in receiving care, factors important to them in care, examples of (good/bad) practice and, finally, similarities/differences between dementia in people from the majority ethnic population and minority ethnic elderly using an "indicators of well being" list (Kitwood and Bredin, 1992).

- *Carers* – the issues concerning carers and the recommendations and areas of improvement considered as important now and in the future, as observed by managers of organisations interviewed. In the results this section will be considered separately from organisations and professionals and supplemented by two case studies which will help shed light on the issues important for carers.

Professionals

The professionals (20) interviewed included GP's, psychogeriatricians/psychiatrists, CPN's and other psychiatric nurses, psychologists, social workers, and other health staff (*e.g.* physiotherapists). This questionnaire was basically similar, albeit more terse, in strategy to that used with organisations. Thus, after brief background questions professionals were asked whether they thought any specific issues related to ethnic minorities with dementia, what difficulties they experienced, how they overcame these difficulties and what they thought would aid them in providing care for this group, and what they considered to be good/bad practice.

Analysis

Data for the organisation interviews will be presented, where appropriate, for the two types of organisation separately, although at times together. Data from professionals will predominantly be presented as a whole although this is an eclectic group including both health and social services staff, as well as being located in various locations – community, hospital wards and nursing homes. Some references will be made to this in the results.

Results And Discussion

1. Organisations

There were 8 day centres and 4 residential homes in this data set. The following results are based on replies from all 12 organisations unless the number of replies is otherwise stated.

General. Both types of organisation provided various services which overlapped to a considerable degree. Thus, both organised activities, provided health provisions and respite services. However, the nature of these categories of services differed which probably reflects the two different types of organisation and resources available to each.

Characteristics. Although all organisations focused on and provided care for minority ethnic older people, these were not a homogenous group. Thus, ten of the twelve organisations had a number of minority ethnic groups that they catered for, who spoke a number of languages and came from different faith backgrounds. The two remaining organisations were both residential homes which catered for Jewish and Polish elder's, respectively.

Referral's. Most of the referral's to both types of organisation came approximately equally from GP's (8), families (10), service users (8) and social workers (6). The surprising finding here may be the referral's from families since it suggests that in the communities served by these organisations knowledge and awareness of dementia may be high. However, it is more likely to reflect frustrations, tensions and difficulties experienced by ethnic minority families with elderly demented relatives, leading them to seek help without understanding or being aware of dementia per se (see below).

How dementia is perceived by families and carers. The view expressed in the last paragraph is borne out by how families and carers themselves understand dementia.

(i) Families. The eight responses from day centres revealed a lack of understanding expressed by minority ethnic families with elderly relatives suffering from dementia. For six respondents these ranged from dementia being a "part of growing old" or "going crazy", not wanting to acknowledge the problem or finding it a burden, to an obvious complete incomprehension of the disease since one respondent suggested it would be "easier too understand if a physical cause could be identified such as stroke".

This latter comment is interesting since a number of professionals suggested that minority ethnic elderly with dementia would more often present as suffering from somatic complaints. May be minority ethnic groups need to be made more aware of somatic complaints commonly associated with dementia or at least that such complaints may be more complex than appreciated – particularly since this may help in earlier diagnosis of the disease. It is known that dementia is diagnosed later in minority ethnic groups compared to those from the majority population (see 2. Professionals below). Families also blamed the demented person for being self-deficient (1 respondent) or openly confessed to a lack of understanding (1 respondent).

Similar views from minority ethnic families were found when interviewing residential homes. Namely, that families tended to play down the problem or indeed refused to visit so as not to see the 'state' of the elderly relative – e.g. avoid "seeing mum screaming". More generally, staff at these homes made it clear that minority ethnic families had little understanding of the problem and found it frustrating.

(ii) Carers. Three responses from day centres emphasized that minority older persons with dementia needed to be supported, whereas another 3 respondents thought that supporting the families was important. The importance of one-to-one

care was also emphasized by 2 respondents, although this may reflect persons who are in the latter stages of the disease and who require constant help. Importance was also attached to the need for bilingual carers (2 respondents) and the need for professional carers with a knowledge of the persons lifestyle (4 responses). It was also clear that training amongst carers was an issue since 4 respondents suggested that professional carers needed to understand more about the demented persons state of health, how to deal with certain aspects of the disease such as wandering, and how to involve the demented person more so as to reduce isolation. Thus, carers in this setting need to both understand the disease better and its management, as well as be more aware of the needs of minority ethnic people with dementia.

In residential homes carers were aware of the special needs/requirements of minority ethnic people with dementia. This view of carers working in a residential home for minority ethnic elderly is expected. This is because the home is trying to meet the needs of minority ethnic elderly with dementia and specific types of carers are recruited to provide for this need. Thus, there was no reference to requiring more knowledge on the lifestyle of the person with dementia or the need for bilingual professional carers as with day centres. Instead three respondents mentioned the importance of physical care (hygiene, safety etc.) and mental stimulation.

Diagnosis. Professionals making the diagnosis for dementia in all the organisations were distributed as follows: GP's (3), psychogeriatricians (5), other psychiatrists (2), neurologists (3) and CPN's (1). There are obvious conflicts here since each of these professionals are likely to define/diagnose dementia differently. Psycho-geriatricians and psychiatrists will use standard clinical tests to determine cognitive deficits, psychiatric symptoms and behavioural disturbances, whereas a neurologist will emphasize impaired reflexes, extrapyramidal signs and myoclonus. Furthermore, diagnosis from GP's and, possibly, CPN's may be less specific than these other professionals (Wallin and Blennow, 1992). For minority ethnic elderly the problem is exacerbated since many clinical tests/rating scales may be inappropriate and neurological signs may differ (Gurland et al., 1995). For example, although the MMSE is frequently used by these professionals in testing the cognitive faculties of a person, research clearly shows that this test, amongst others, is inappropriate for different ethnic groups as it stands (Bohnstedt et al., 1994). Some studies have adapted commonly used assessment scales such as the MMSE for different communities (e.g. Spanish and Hindi) and have found that not only is this difficult, but that at times some questions have to be completely changed to make them culturally-sensitive (Ganguli et al., 1995; Loewenstein et al., 1993). Finally, it is also unclear how much cross-talk there is between these professionals.

Care plans: adequacy and issues. Although care plans had been identified in replies from seven day centres only 2 respondents felt these were adequate, whereas four respondents said they were inadequate. One respondent indicated that care plans would be adequate if resources were available. Six of the respondents emphasized that whereas services were available they were culturally inappropriate, an issue that arises again amongst professionals (see below). These respondents also emphasized the lack of resources in terms of care worker availability and little home help. As suggested above in the discussion on diagnostic issues, a further exacerbating problem appeared to be inadequate co-ordination or cross-talk between hospitals, social services and day centres.

Residential centre respondents not surprisingly said that care plans were adequate. As residential centres did not appear to have financial problems to the same extent as day centres, issues concentrated more on the persons well-being. In this regard the idea of 'stimulating' the patient was emphasized – carers were not simply satisfied in the dementia sufferer appearing to take part in music and songs, but were more interested in ascertaining what made the patient 'tick'. One-to-one care was important for determining this. Such a person-centred approach may be particularly useful for ethnic minorities since in group-centred approaches cultural, religious and spiritual needs may not easily be identified – e.g. when using a group reminiscence approach to care.

The above may suggest that minority ethnic person with dementia and their families may benefit more from a residential placement. Not only do day centres have financial difficulties, but they are also involved in wider issues with various bodies – these factors may detract from the issues and care of the sufferer him/herself. However, the important setting of day centres within the community and their ability to access various services can also be of benefit to the demented person and his/her family (see below). This implies that the difficulties facing day centres outlined above need to be addressed and their position improved if they are to continue providing care for minority ethnic people with dementia.

Care plans: approaches, difficulties and how they are overcome.

(i) Approaches. In both day centres and residential homes a wide variety of care approaches were used. Thus, in day centres reality orientation, activities/stimulation (audio/video, games, arts and crafts, keep-fit and tai chi), environmental approaches, person-centred and reminiscence approaches were all used (Fig. 1). In addition there were alternative therapies including natural healing and prayers, which may be particularly pertinent to minority ethnic groups within the context of using resources and the communities people come from.

Although care in residential homes used the same approaches as day centres, with the addition of validation therapy, there appeared to be more caution in their use (Fig. 1). For example, whilst reminiscence work was useful it had to be used with care so as not to trigger "*bad memories*". Two of the residential homes were unaware of what a person-centred approach was, and this seems to be a problem of terminology used since one-to-one care was used in these homes (see above). One respondent complained of "*theories not working*" and having to develop "*home-grown*" therapies as alternatives. This suggests that some of the care approaches commonly used are not appropriate for ethnic minorities and that so-called 'home-grown' approaches should be investigated to ascertain whether they can be positively transferred to other centres/homes and the mainstream.

(ii) Difficulties. For day centres these included resources (finance and staff), professional services not being responsive to the cultural needs of users and, notably, family difficulties. Families would not accept the illness, felt guilty because it was *their* duty to look after the demented person at home, were unwilling to get outside help, and in one case interference from family members not directly involved in the care of the dementia sufferer became problematic. Cultural factors, personal limits in information and development activities were also seen as difficulties (Fig. 2). Residential homes showed a similar distribution in the types of difficulties encountered although less problems with professional services and development activities. By contrast to day centres, all residential staff had difficulties due to personal limits in information about the disease itself (Fig. 2). To the extent that these homes specifically care for minority ethnic elderly this latter finding is surprising. However, it may reflect the fact that whilst these homes are specific for minority ethnic elderly they are not specific to people with dementia. Thus, there is a mix of elderly people being cared for, only some of whom have dementia. In this regard day centres may be more useful and appropriate for minority ethnic people with dementia since they are able to access specific services which cater for dementia patients.

(iii) Overcoming difficulties. In trying to overcome these difficulties only 3 of the 8 day centres said they had managed this - this reflects the greater overall difficulties encountered by day centres as opposed to residential homes (see below and Fig. 2). Approaches included attaining more information from consultants and attending lectures on Alzheimer's disease, increased practical training, more inter-agency co-operation, improving staff-staff relations (supporting each other) and staff-client relations (empathising with the demented person, helping in family difficulties and making families aware of services available to them), and increased resources (bilingual staff to help the demented person at hospitals *etc.*). The residential homes that answered this question said that they had overcome difficulties, again using similar methods as day centres.

In contrast to how organisations had overcome difficulties (Fig. 2), Figure 3 outlines the type and extent of support that organisations *actually* feel they need to overcome their difficulties in caring for minority ethnic people with dementia. Of interest was the number of organisations emphasizing the need for committed staff and a good balance between staff who were bilingual and those who spoke only English.

Barriers to services faced by ethnic minorities and how they have been overcome. Every organisation agreed that their were barriers. In the case of day centres there were seven different identifiable barriers. Although language and communication, lack of resources (*e.g.* assessment facilities) and information, and the stigma of the illness being a form of madness are obvious highlights, the barriers extended to this group by professionals is particularly worrying. General practitioners were unable to explain the illness and often sent people home, hospitals and social services departments appeared to have 'no time' for patients, and the methods and tools used by professionals were inappropriate and their attitudes were interpreted as racist. Moreover, the complexity of the system itself was seen as a barrier since services are scattered rather than housed under one roof, and this in combination with a lack of communication between different service providers posed multiple hurdles, exacerbating the scale of the problem for vulnerable people. It also suggests that there are no simple answers, whether practical or otherwise, to providing adequate care for minority ethnic elderly with dementia.

As expected their were fewer barriers perceived by residential homes, but they included communication, culture (the notion that the client was 'begging' was difficult to alleviate) and staff, since they did not share the cultural/linguistic background as the person(s) with dementia or viewed them through stereotypes.

As regards overcoming barriers both types of organisation appear to be taking appropriate steps. In common, both are using equal opportunities legislation in the interests of the person with dementia. They are raising awareness and explaining dementia 'personally' by attaining more information from experts and Alzheimer's disease associations, and having more contact with families. In addition day centres are doing outreach work in the community and acting as advocates for sufferers. The suggestion from many day centres was that voluntary community organisations should be involved more, partly because they are trusted by minority ethnic groups but also because they can act as a 'one-stop-shop' where minorities can access various services and thereby obviate the complexities of the system.

Cultural and communication considerations and developments in the care of ethnic minorities with dementia. A recurring theme was the difficulty of communication and cultural barriers regarding caring for minority ethnic elderly with dementia. Factors organisations felt should be considered included having professionals who understood the persons culture, language and background. From a practical perspective respondents highlighted the following as important steps to meeting cultural needs – using life story techniques (reminiscence), understanding the persons moods, addressing them by personal names, food (*e.g.* Caribbean) and music (*e.g.* reggae) should be culture specific, separate rooms for men and women which is important in some cultures, having a client charter, and the importance of a wide range of services for both the demented person and their families. However, these practical cultural needs were difficult to meet due to a lack of resources for staffing, training and carrying out outreach work, the short-term nature of funding and competition for these funds, reluctance of families in allowing their relative to be cared for by professionals rather than a family member, and the difficulty staff face in having to think about every single daily activity since simply transferring practice used with the majority population was not appropriate. This staffing issue would strongly suggest that more minority ethnic staff are required.

Future development. It is clear from the above that there is a two-way process in this area. Not only does the world of dementia need to *see* ethnicity as a significant aspect in the care of minority ethnic elderly with dementia, but minority ethnic people need to *recognise* dementia as a disease. For example, the former relates to professionals and health and social services to recognise that adaptations and investigations are needed if they are to provide adequate care for minority ethnic elderly with dementia – particularly with regard to the importance of respect and religious/spiritual indicators of relative well-being which scored highly amongst a list of indicators by the organisations in this study (Kitwood and Bredin, 1992). By contrast, organisations catering for minority ethnic people with dementia need to consider the combined forces of competence in ethnicity and dementia: it is not only a matter of having minority ethnic staff (whether that be nurses in a nursing home, social work/ care staff at day centres or relatives of the person with dementia) to care for minority ethnic elderly with dementia, but that this staff also require training and understanding of the disease itself if the quality of life of the person is to improve.

Summary. The following highlight the main findings from this study on organisations:

- Language – dementia suffers and their families who do not speak English face problems at every stage when trying to get care.

- Information – minority ethnic families are unable to communicate with care professionals or are not able to access information on what services are available to them.

- Culture – many cultures fail to recognise that dementia is an illness. Because of this issues are not addressed and dementia is accepted as an inevitable part of growing old. Cultural problems also account for families tending to look after the person with dementia themselves and not trying to get outside help. This leads to the person coming to the attention of care professionals later in the illness.

- Complexity of the care system – minority ethnic people with multi-faceted illnesses such as dementia who are, in addition, disadvantaged by language and the cultural stigma associated with disease in old age, face huge problems in negotiating a very complex system which involves several agencies with their own methods of working.

- Funding for care provision – the inadequate and short-term nature of funding is a particular problem for day centres and voluntary organisations, which impedes their ability to provide services. Since day centres may for various reasons (see above) be better placed to provide care for minority ethnic elderly with dementia than residential centres, this is yet another barrier that they face.

- Specialist organisations – analysing the current context of care for minority ethnic elderly and the critical position of minority ethnic organisations in providing this care, a recommendation for further specialist organisations as an area of development appears to be a sensible pragmatic solution. These organisations are already on the ground providing this care. Not only do such organisations recognise the current unmet need in these communities but it is estimated that in the near future there will be higher numbers of older people from such communities (see country profile section).

- Training, and materials development – it is clear from these findings that organisations want training ('specialist advice and support' in working with professionals) and 'appropriate' resources to support existing materials in how to care for people with dementia and to understand more about the clients culture and background.

- Policy and Research – all organisations regarded these two areas equally worthy of immediate development.

2. Professionals

Issues related to minority ethnic elderly with dementia

Figure 4 outlines the main issues that professionals cited as important. Twelve respondents cited diagnosis as a major issue. The reasons for this were that professionals found it difficult to diagnose dementia in minority ethnic people because both families and professionals clashed 'culturally'. Thus, professionals found it difficult to delineate between what they considered to be 'dementia symptoms' and what the family considered was 'normal behaviour', given their cultural norms. However, not in all cases was this behaviour culture specific, and as with the findings from organisations, families accepted symptoms/behaviour of the relative as a normal part of old age. Again this suggests that minority ethnic communities need to be made more aware of dementia symptoms.

The other major issue was that of communication – 17 respondents saw this as an important issue. The specific issues were not simply related to professionals and minority ethnic elderly with dementia not speaking the same language, *e.g.* Chinese patients not speaking English. The person with dementia often spoke in his/her mother tongue even though he/she could speak English. This was not just a reversion to their first language – patients would often become irrational making it difficult for both the families and translators, as well as professionals, to understand what they were trying to say. Whilst irrational behaviour may seem to be a symptom commonly encountered with dementia/ageing and manifest in the general population, two aspects of this issue are important for minority ethnic elderly with dementia. Firstly, a number of professionals felt that minority ethnic dementia sufferers were at times trying to hide their symptoms behind irrational use of language (*i.e.* a mixture of both English and their mother tongue). Secondly, the person with dementia had difficulty expressing him/herself – again this was not simply due to the person reverting to his/her mother tongue or use of 'irrational language'; instead it may reflect the fact that minority ethnic people are referred later (8 professionals cited this as a problem) and were therefore diagnosed later in the illness (12 respondents) than white patients. An inability to express and explain oneself becomes progressively worse in the latter stages of the disease (*i.e.* dysphasia, dysarthria, perseveration and the form, speed and content of thoughts and speech, Wattis, 1989). This is likely to exacerbate the difficulties professionals have in caring for minority ethnic older persons with dementia.

Such a continual cycle needs initially to be broken at input – the person with dementia needs to be referred earlier and this means (a) raising awareness and understanding in families and communities who tend to care for the sufferer at home and who are reluctant to refer them until they are no longer able to cope (8 respondents) and (b) professionals need more training and resources to diagnose minority ethnic elderly with dementia.

At the output stage (*i.e.* care), professionals need more training and support in understanding how to care and what type of care is required by minority ethnic elderly – ten respondents said that type of care was an issue. Specific comments from professionals included the need for minority ethnic carers, involving relatives more as they appeared to be marginalised and when they were involved it was only in moments of crisis. Involving relatives only at times of crisis is likely to exacerbate guilt which stems from their feeling that 'they are expected to provide the care' for an elderly relative. Furthermore, although minority ethnic carers are needed in caring for minority ethnic elderly with dementia, professionals also emphasized that carers needed to be educated in providing physical care and medication, regardless of their ethnicity. This point was also raised in the organisation responses and needs to be considered more closely.

Difficulties experienced working with ethnic minorities with dementia

Fifteen respondents listed different types and degrees of difficulties they had encountered in working with minority ethnic elderly with dementia. For example, three respondents said that carers felt that the person was "*mad*" – this no doubt reflects a complete inability to understand the needs of a minority ethnic person suffering from dementia and the lack of training and awareness on the part of the carer. This is verified by three respondents saying that 'cultural features' were not understood and presumed to be dementia related – *e.g.* the swaying/rocking movement which is a normal part of Muslim prayer. One respondent replied that whilst carers were aware that there was a problem they needed more information, particularly from GP's who would provide a diagnosis but no explanation as too what this diagnosis meant. Three respondents also expressed concern regarding the value of activities and stimulation as a part of care since it did not always include all participants - *e.g.* "*cake-making was only enjoyed by women*"; "*only half the participants joined in at a sing-a-long*". This suggests that a person-centred approach may be more appropriate for certain types of care given to ethnic minorities with dementia. One respondent complained about a lack of services generally for this group.

Solutions to these difficulties

Eleven respondents gave details of solutions they had attempted to use in overcoming difficulties (Fig. 5). Most of this revolved around language barriers, namely learning the language or using interpreters for persons with dementia. However, as shown above communication and language are not simple isolated issues, but are instead part of a more complex problem which reflects family issues, 'cultural features', referral's, diagnosis and stage of the disease. This emphasizes the fact that verbal language is just one aspect of communication, and that non-verbal communication is a major issue for minority ethnic groups.

Other solutions included increasing family participation – providing them with more information and working with families directly (4 respondents). Learning from other staff members was also cited by one respondent.

Requirements/suggestions to improve practice

In contrast to Figure 5 which shows the type of solutions attempted by professionals, Figure 6 lists requirements which professionals suggested would *actually* improve practice. Although 16 respondents commented on this issue and only 11 on the solutions issue, some comparisons can be made between the two to give an idea of the shortfall between solutions used and what professionals perceived as being necessary requirements that would improve practice. Immediately apparent is the longer list of requirements as compared to solutions used. Particularly interesting was the finding that whereas approximately 55 percent of professionals had attempted to learn the persons language or, more commonly, used interpreters (Fig 5), only 25 percent perceived this as a requirement that would improve care practice (Fig. 6). This suggests, and is borne out by Figure 6, that other requirements are more important in care practice and that language barriers are not necessarily the most important factor as is commonly proposed (Patel, 1990). Therefore, the use of translators and bilingual staff is important in overcoming language barriers, but this alone is not sufficient since such staff are only likely to be needed at "*critical times*". By contrast, whereas only 36.4 percent of professionals had involved families more in care practice, over 60 percent cited this as being an important aspect in improving care (compare Figs. 5 and 6). This suggests that involving the families of minority ethnic older people with dementia in the care process may be an important option in the future, and that more resources should be channelled this way – as one professional said, "*more resources should be committed to this area and funding for such projects tends to be short term*".

More important than both language- and family- orientated solutions was training. All 16 respondents said further training would improve practice. Specific examples of training needs included:

- being better informed about dementia and recognizing behaviours associated with it, *e.g.* wandering;

- recognising vascular symptoms; this is an issue recently raised regarding elderly Afro-Caribbean's who had a higher rate of hypertension and diabetes than elderly white's (Richards, 1996);

- professionals wanted information on cultural/religious practices which they felt may impact on a clients behaviour and daily routine.

In addition to information being available to professionals as part of training, over 80 percent of professionals said that information, particularly in the form of materials (over 65 percent of respondents), should also be disseminated to communities to increase awareness and reduce fear of the illness; thereby helping professionals devise more activities for the person with dementia by receiving input from minority ethnic communities. In aiding this process of awareness in the community and to identify the illness earlier, 50 percent of professionals said that specialist ethnic minority workers would be needed to improve practice (Fig. 6). To a certain degree it is encouraging that all respondents themselves felt that they needed more training (see Fig. 6 and discussion above), whereas only 50 percent suggested that a specialist ethnic minority worker would be important. This implies that professionals are aware of their own short-comings in providing dementia care for minority ethnic users/patients and would like to improve this. It is also obvious that a specialist minority ethnic worker may actually aid this process.

Examples of good and bad practice in care provision

Examples of good practice that professionals had encountered appeared to focus on solutions they themselves had used – including using interpreters and recruiting bilingual staff (8 respondents), and involving the family more in the formulation of the care package (6 respondents). Community psychiatric nurses suggested that home visits were particularly useful in involving family members in care. Trying to understand the culture of the client was cited as good practice; as in one example where staff understood and accepted the Muslim practice of washing oneself several times a day. Learning on the job was also seen as good practice – *e.g.* one respondent reported allowing a demented person a cigarette after taking advice from the community psychiatric nurse who knew more about the culture, having visited the family of the client at home, than the professional in question. The method of learning on the job could be one that is usefully incorporated as it can lead to a 'snowball' effect resulting in better care for ethnic minorities. However, it needs to have some structure as it becomes dangerous if only certain views are passed on between professionals leading to 'stagnant ideas/thinking'.

Examples of bad practice were cited on an individual basis with little consensus between professionals, unlike with the examples of good practice discussed above. This may imply that there will be considerable difficulty in excising bad practice. Table 6 below summarizes examples of bad practice alongside those considered to be examples of good practice. Numbers in parentheses indicate the number of respondents.

Table 6: Examples of Good and Bad Practice cited by Professionals

Good practice	Bad practice
1. Using interpreters and having bilingual staff (8)	1. Not communicating well with the person with dementia and their family (2)
2. Involving relatives in the formulation of a care package and visiting the person with dementia at home (6)	2. Not providing support for families (1)
3. Professionals learning on the job (2)	3. Ignoring cultural practice of user/patient and not incorporating them into their daily routine (1)
4. Trying to understand the culture of the user/ patient(1)	4. Having racist staff (1)
	5. Not resolving conflicts between persons with dementia(1)
	6. Inadequate funding (1)
	7. Misdiagnosis of condition (1)

How the ethnicity of users/ patients has affected care plans

Only 8 professionals answered this question, making it difficult to reach a valid conclusion on this issue. Respondents cited how the clients language (2 respondents), culture (1 respondent) and background (1 respondent) had influenced their care plans. Four professionals said ethnicity had not made a difference to their care plans because compassion, kindness and understanding were common attributes in dealing with all people with dementia. However, as is apparent under the Methodology section the professionals were an eclectic group. Closer inspection of the questionnaires showed that all four respondents who said ethnicity had not altered their care plans were non-psychiatric professionals. Understandably psychiatric staff were more *au fait* with the issues at hand, but this suggests that non-psychiatric health and social services staff require more training, understanding and awareness of care issues involved with minority ethnic elderly with dementia.

Summary

The following highlight the main findings from this study on professionals:

- Diagnosis – professionals said that diagnosing dementia in minority ethnic people was difficult due to cultural differences and late referrals.

- Training – professionals said they needed more training to better understand the cultural/religious aspects in caring for minority ethnic elderly with dementia, as well as for improving diagnosis.

- Communication – whilst interpreters and bilingual staff were useful in verbally communicating with minority ethnic users/patients, thus aiding in the care process, professionals were aware that non-verbal communication was an important aspect – specialist ethnic minority workers may be useful in this regard.

- Information – professionals themselves needed more information on dementia. However, it was also suggested that more information, particularly in the form of materials, needed to be disseminated amongst minority ethnic communities to raise awareness and reduce fear of dementia.

- Support – professionals suggested more support for minority ethnic families who had a relative with dementia. This would also aid professionals in devising more appropriate care plans.

- Care – it was suggested that involving families more in the formulation of the demented relatives care plan, and the use of minority ethnic carers would improve care for the dementia sufferer.

3. Minority Ethnic Carers

Some of the following data on minority ethnic carers was generated from interviewing managers of ethnic minority organisations using the same questionnaire on organisations discussed above. Some such organisations themselves run family carers' support groups while others are in constant contact with individual carers. Hence the organisations are in a good position to have some understanding of key issues affecting carers. In addition there are two case studies given below from research by Gina Netto (1996).

Work done with carers

Day centres in particular were increasingly supporting minority ethnic carers by encouraging them to talk about their problems, providing emotional support and social contacts which have led to some carers support networks being established (including one in Punjabi which recently ceased). Carers were also encouraged to use respite care services. Residential homes were providing information on respite care and benefits to carers, and also organising sessions for carers to express their emotions.

Issues related to minority ethnic carers

Five day centres recognised that carers needed more information about what help was available to them – "*many are trying to be self-sufficient*", the need to encourage more carer groups so as to avoid isolation, and the importance of providing more services for carers. Employment opportunities were also an issue for minority ethnic carers once care work was over.

Both the work being done by organisations with carers and the issues relating to minority ethnic carers are summarized in Table 7 below. The numbers in parentheses are the number of respondents.

Table 7: Carers issues

Work done with carers	Issues relating to minority ethnic carers
1. Training work (3)	1. Information to carers about help available needs to be increased (5)
2. Carers were given information and encouraged to use respite, as well as details of benefits they were entitled to (2)	2. Carers are trying to be self-sufficient (10)
3. Creating a carers support network (2)	3. More respite care services were needed for carers (10)
4. Carers were being encouraged to communicate their problems (12)	4. Lack of employment opportunities when care work is over (10).
5. Organisations are providing emotional support and social contacts for carer's (12).	

Case studies on dementia sufferers: minority ethnic carers

(We acknowledge Gina Netto, Heriot Watt University, Edinburgh for writing these two case studies for the *CNEOPSA* Project).

Case Study 1

Background. Mr and Mrs A are of Pakistani origin and are both in poor health. Whilst Mrs A suffers from high blood pressure, diabetes and poor eyesight, she is the sole carer for Mr A. Mr A has been diagnosed as suffering from dementia and displays the classic cognitive (difficulty following conversation, not recognising people and repeating the same question), neurological (reaching, stretching and picking up things, as well as problems with sight and speech) and associated psychiatric/behavioural disturbances (depression, aggression and anxiety). Mrs A describes Mr A as suffering from 'an attack on his mind'. In describing how caring for

Mr A has affected her, Mrs A says, "*I forget myself, what I am, because I have to look after him every minute, every second*".

Mrs A has cared for Mr A for six years with no family support. Care includes dressing and bathing, physical help with walking, paper work (dealing with bills), household chores, keeping him company and helping him obtain medical support. On occasion a neighbour of Pakistani origin, who speaks English, takes Mr A to the doctor.

Health and social services. In the past 18 months Mr A has had 'brain X-rays' and been visited at home once a week by a professional to 'stimulate his mind'. Mrs A feels satisfied with the health services and comments on how Mr A's language is improving (the professional is probably a speech therapist). In addition Mrs A has had a visit from a social worker and now receives home help three times a week which gives her a break. However, she is unhappy with the frequent change in staff.

Support Mrs A requires

(1)   Mrs A says she needs help bathing Mr A, and that the person doing this should be white and male so that Mr A can speak English and feel less embarrassed in being cared for by someone "*who did not have a brown skin*". Equipment that would aid Mrs A to bathe Mr A would also be useful, although she is unsure what equipment she should get nor how to obtain it.

(2)   Someone to take Mr A to the doctor, hairdressers, and out for walks would be helpful as Mrs A is uncomfortable with him going out alone.

(3)   Mrs A said that she could not use the 'meals on wheels' service because the food they eat is halal food – she was unaware that this could be provided.

(4)   She also wanted Mr A to attend a day centre twice a week but was concerned about halal food at such a centre.

(5)   Although, as mentioned above, Mrs A had been visited by a social worker it is apparent from the above that she is not aware of all the services, including financial assistance, available to her.

(6)   Mrs A would like to attend an Asian lunch club for older people, but has had problems finding transport for herself and Mr A.

Information Mrs A requires

Mrs A's main source of information is her Pakistani neighbour. She has expressed an interest in obtaining information on financial help, as well as other information in the form of leaflets in her mother tongue – *e.g.* she wants information on practical tasks such as lifting.

Asked about anything else she wanted to add about her caring experiences, Mrs A replied "*sometimes I feel helpless, I want to die, but I cannot die*".

Case Study 2

Background. Mr B is Chinese, in his sixties and describes his health as "quite poor". He suffers from dizzy spells and blackouts. Although in bad health he has been caring for his wife Mrs B, who shows signs typical of dementia – repeating the same question, difficulty recognising people except very close friends, difficulty in following a conversation, frequently forgets what she is talking about and strays in conversation, often says hurtful and insulting things to people, hides things in one place and then removes them and hides them in another place (thus, when these things go 'missing' and she cannot find them she accuses others of stealing them), is aggressive and forgets when she has been so, and suffers from depression. Mrs B has been on medication for 10 years, and apart from difficulty in walking her physical health is good. However, when Mr B suffers dizzy spells/blackouts Mrs B cares for him.

Mr B describes his wife as suffering from "*a mental health problem*" and said that she had previously been admitted to a psychiatric hospital. Mr B's perception was that mental health problems were difficult to cure and that people with these problems were always confused.

Mr B gave up work to care for his wife and is now totally reliant upon benefits – income support and disability living allowance. He carries out all household chores – he does not allow Mrs B to do the cooking as she is likely to leave the gas or water taps on. He only leaves her alone to do shopping. His neighbours, who live in the same sheltered housing project for elderly Chinese people as they do, sometimes visit too keep Mrs B company. He has to always accompany Mrs B when she leaves the house because she is likely to get lost.

Health and social services. The only medical service Mr B is receiving is that of a general practitioner who is familiar with Mrs B's condition. Mr B felt that he had been looking after Mrs B for so long that he had enough knowledge of her condition - presumably enough to be able to care for her full-time. For example, if he irritated her she got worse, whereas if he was pleasant and occupied her mind then her mental condition was better and she was unlikely to complain or be awkward.

However, at the time of this interview Mr and Mrs B were both attending a lunch club for elderly Chinese people once a fortnight and receiving 'meals on wheels' three times a week. He was satisfied with both services since the lunch club gave Mrs B a chance to talk and to see more people, whereas the 'meals on wheels' service lessened the burden of cooking on himself.

Mr B reported that neither he nor Mrs B felt isolated or bored as they were living in the sheltered housing scheme for elderly Chinese people, and were also visited by friends from church and the lunch club. He was also satisfied with the apartment because its small size enabled him to be more aware of his wife in the kitchen.

Support Mr B requires

(1)   Mr B has expressed a desire for the lunch club sessions to be extended for longer hours and the 'meals on wheels' service to be provided more often – 5 days per week.

(2)   He would also like to meet regularly with other carers but added that someone else would have to be with Mrs B while he attended such meetings.

(3)   Mr B said that if Mrs B had someone to talk to her mind would not 'wander off' so much.   He wanted a service which could cater for this – *i.e.* someone to converse with Mrs B two or three time a week.   Since Mrs B could only speak Hakka this person would have to speak in this language, or may be Cantonese.

(4)   He also expressed a desire for Mrs B to attend a day centre once a week, emphasizing that the staff should speak the same language as her and that the food should be what Mrs B is used too.

(5)   He responded positively to the availability of crisis support services, again stressing the language and food factors mentioned above.   He also stressed that staff should ensure that Mrs B does not leave the premises.

(6)   He added that any form of financial help would be useful, but that in his experience this was difficult to attain.

(7)   He said that in the event of his death Mrs B would have no alternative but to go to a residential home.

Information Mr B requires

Mr B admitted that he did not have enough information about health services which were available to him, not where to obtain information on these services.   His main source of information was a voluntary organisation which served the elderly Chinese community and the bilingual warden at the sheltered housing project.   He expressed a desire to obtain information on financial help he was entitled to, and the services provided by the Health and Social Services Department's.   He was also interested in this information in the form of an audio cassette in his mother tongue.

Summary

It is clear from the above that whilst some efforts are being made to help ethnic minority carers to maintain an adequate level of care for themselves and their patient, and that organisations recognise their needs (Table 7) – not all their needs are being met as is borne out by the two case studies. Thus, both Mrs A and Mr B have extensively long lists regarding the support they require, and neither of them appears to have enough information on the disease itself, the type and the range of services available to them or the financial benefits they are entitled to. Indeed, the range of health services both carers receive appear to be meagre compared to what they are entitled to. Furthermore, it is apparent that both carers are trying to be self-sufficient. Clearly, these case studies highlight some of the issues relating to ethnic minority carers listed in Table 7. Particularly important is the fact that both carers are very specific and aware of the type of support/help they require – which may well be as a result of their engagement with minority ethnic older organisations. This vindicates what both the organisations and professionals said (see Parts 1 and 2 above) – that families and relatives as carers of ethnic minority patients with dementia should be given greater support and information so that they can be involved more in the formulation of a care plan, thus leading to the improved care of the patient as well as the well-being of the carer.

SECTION 2: The Management of Care

1. Introduction

In Section 1, we explained our approach to the UK study, presented the key findings and analysed them in their context. This section describes how we should interpret these important findings and the recommendations that emerge from them regarding the area of ethnicity and welfare. In considering this we also need to first ask how we should regard the person with dementia – the main focus of our subject.

To begin then....

> Time Present and Time Past
> Are both perhaps present in time future
> And time future contained in time past

> *T. S. Eliot*
> *Four Quartets*

Once *You* were somebody...Now *You* are no more .. a category... a body with no mind...but there are memories of the Past to use for care in the Present ..to generate a sense of *Being* in the here ..*Now* in Present and for the Future.
"Once Dementia existed only as a clinical category...progress has been made in a short time regarding subjectivity of the person with dementia" (Kitwood 1997, pg. 70).

Once *You* were somebody...Now *You* have several labels: a minority, an immigrant, a demented minority....and the Past concepts of "us" and "them" will define in the Present "who should receive what form of care, if any,...they look after their own, don't they?"

What do we see... *Who* do we see... *How* do we see... *Why* do we see... *When* do we see... *Where* do we see....
Do we see... the *person* ... with *dementia* ... from a *minority ethnic* background....
... *Who* cares?

Answers to such questions are important if care in the future is to progress beyond past and present methods. This is particularly pertinent regarding dementia which comprises both neurological and social-psychological changes and strikes indiscriminately. Basic questions can sometimes be lost in the plethora of literature on dementia/Alzheimer's disease. As the great poet Kabir says, "*To whom shall I go to learn about my Beloved? As you never may find the forest if you ignore the tree, so He may never be found in abstractions*" (Tagore, 1915, I.108.XC). To find dementia and not the person is to miss the tree and indeed the forest – the very essence of what we call *being...Humanity.*

Section 1 has provided us with some useful information which can help plan the journey and recognise not only the tree, but also explore its many branches and perhaps the forest itself (*i.e.* the recommendations of professionals and minority organisations). Our approach was not to fragment specific aspects but to distil learning from practice "on the ground". After all when a person with dementia appears at any one of the organisations we interviewed, they cannot reply: *"wait we have no appropriate diagnostic instruments or materials......or what was that about E2020?"* They have to respond as best they can, amid various demands and constraints. Indeed this is what our findings in Section 1 show – the recommendations made by organisations and professionals give us a good grounding on the appropriate type of work that needs to be done now and in the future, although we do not suggest that answers to specific questions (and there are many) are unimportant.

2. The Aims: "Seeing the Tree..."

From Section 1 it is apparent that we need to consider three main factors in the management of care:

- the carers;

- the professionals; and the

- capacity of minority organisations to respond to care for people with dementia.

The analysis of these three factors is in reverse order to the data that was generated from them so as to provide some continuity from the previous section and to begin as close to the demented person as possible – hence we begin with the carers, both the data generated from our questionnaire with minority ethnic organisations and the two case studies.

Kitwood and Bredin's (1992) list of 'Indicators of relative well-being in dementia were identified by minority ethnic organisations in our study, and we can regard these indicators as the standards which they aim to achieve in the process of planning and delivering their services. Similarly, achieving these indicators of well-being can be extended to professional and family carers. As these indicators are a basis by which we can measure how good/bad care or services are they are listed completely below:

- The assertion or desire of will

- The ability to experience and express a range of emotions (both 'positive' and 'negative')

- Initiation of social contact

- Affectional warmth

- Social sensitivity

- Self-respect

- Acceptance of other dementia sufferers

- Humour

- Creativity and self-expression

- Showing evident pleasure

- Helpfulness

- Relaxation

All respondents agreed with this list as being relevant to the care of minority ethnic older people with dementia. In addition they qualified this list by placing particular significance on religion and spirituality in daily care. This is not surprising since many aspects of 'appropriate practice' are culture-bound, regardless of socio-economic, religious or spiritual factors. So in organisations we interviewed, celebration of festivals, observance of particular religious customs - prayers or daily communication of parables or proverbs – all connect individuals to faith, philosophy and spirituality irrespective of the individuals' level of religiosity. As part of being 'in the community' family carers may undertake similar practices at home and/or participate in such events. As Froggatt and Moffitt (1997) state *"For carers too, religious support and spiritual awareness may help to answer some of the difficult questions"*. It is necessary to emphasise however that, given the known use of religious and spiritual practices among our target group (including physical forms of exercise – *e.g.* yoga) and the qualification made above to the list of indicators, it is necessary to explore further how this area of work helps individuals, as this may offer a different perspective in say Reminiscence work.

So how do they, as Family Carers, Professional staff and minority ethnic organisations work to attain the above indicators of well-being in persons with dementia?

3. Family Carers

Although it was beyond the scope of our project to have done an in-depth study of family carers' experience, issues and needs, our brief questions do, however, point to some immediate concerns: (a) minority ethnic day centres recognise the need to support carers who in turn are responding to their services; (b) carers support networks at day centres and respite care within community settings are providing support and direct work with carers. In a general survey on minority ethnic carers in Edinburgh and the Lothians in Scotland, Netto (1996), found that in addition to sharing similar issues to white family carers, minority ethnic carers experienced the effects of 'colour-blind' services once they managed to enter the system of care.

For those outside the system of care, family carers' experiences reflect the barriers in accessing services commonly encountered by minority ethnic older people. Furthermore, they live within the context of racial harassment and discrimination in housing, employment and health and social care services. For example in the government inspection of services for older people with dementia, "*home care was by far the most frequent service on which older people with dementia and their carers relied*" (pg. 7). It would be useful to see how far the implementation of the Carers (Recognition and Services) Act 1995 assesses the needs of carers from our target group. Add to this the concept of 'duty' and its role in care-giving within the family, and we begin to appreciate that even carers with strong personalities could potentially sink into poor care provision, as well as suffer depression and ill-health themselves.

Not surprisingly, minority ethnic centres are aware of the pivotal role played by carers. Indeed, the care provided in the family home represents a considerable saving for the authorities. The critical issue then is how far and effectively can such centres support carers, when they themselves are marginalised due to temporary finance. Moreover, how far the concept of 'duty' decreases the likelihood of carers trying to attain external support is worthy of further examination, as well as the concept's potential for abuse – "*the sons appeared to be enjoying the benefit of her pension*" (Boneham *et al.*, 1997, who looked at mental illness, unmet needs and barriers to services for 71 elderly people from minority ethnic groups in Liverpool).

It may well be that we are looking at this issue of the carer and the family member with dementia from a general White perspective. In essence our examination may need to first consider higher level external factors – poverty in association with poor housing, and fear of safety (Patel, 1990; Boneham *et al.*, 1997) – which prevent the fulfilment of 'duty' in care relationships. Domestic division of labour (often there are multi-carers in the family), roles, beliefs about service beyond oneself and exchange of duties and responsibilities are inextricably linked with the idea of the continuance of family; however, the family itself is facing the socio-economic pressures and demands of modern day living. Improvements in the families socio-economic circumstances with access to welfare services (*e.g.* home care mentioned above) may be the ladder that enables carers to fulfil their 'duty' of caring and thereby benefit the person with dementia. This should not be difficult to understand, and yet the unmet needs and barriers exist on a large scale. As Professor Phillipson from Keele University, who is currently examining the position of the elderly in inner cities, found – the claim for benefits by minority ethnic elders in one London borough was so low, despite the fact that they were entitled to such benefits, that if these entitlements were taken up the group would be "*rich overnight*"!

In short, the carer needs to be recognised, requires specific care training related to dementia, and needs to sustain him/herself. However, improvements in the carers socio-economic position are necessary if this training in care provision is to be effective. If your family is experiencing high levels of unemployment, poverty with poor housing, worries about fuel bills and receives no information on external welfare services, any amount of good training on how to care for a family member with dementia may be of little consequence.

So If we work to realise the well-being indicators for a person with dementia but forget the significant role played by the family carer, then it is akin to seeing a partial tree.....

4. The Professional Carers

It is interesting to find that 15 out of 20 professional respondents expressed difficulties working with minority ethnic people with dementia (see Results and Discussion, Section 1). When examining aspects of their "good practice", cultural considerations constituted a large part of this. However, their recognition of the range of difficulties encountered and solutions considered do not neatly fall into *"let's have a list of food, language and religion"* aspects of culture alone. This is encouraging since the professional carers were from a range of professions and already engaged in working with minority ethnic patients with dementia (see Methodology, Section 1). Such a heightened awareness of gaps in services could be attributed to a series of developments in the health sector. There have been several broad national initiatives led by the NHS Ethnic Health Unit, SHARE at Kings Fund (both now closed), the Department of Health, individual Trusts and Health Boards. In social work, the Central Council for Education and Training in Social Work sets the requirement of competency to work in a multiracial society for a professional qualification in social work in the UK. Moreover, social services/social work departments have supported work, ranging from declaration of equal opportunities policy to concrete developments appropriate for its multi-ethnic client-base.

As we saw earlier in Part 1: The UK country profile, very few developments can be cited in relation to dementia for this target group, but broad initiatives in employment and services can have *knock-on effects* in other areas for professionals and indeed the development of services within a hospital, a nursing home, a residential home or a GP surgery. The encouraging finding from our study is that professional carers recognise their shortcomings and are aware that the problem of minority ethnic elders with dementia is not simple. For those engaged in the field of ethnic relations, this finding is significant since many have struggled to get the issue *"merely on the agenda"*. This therefore is progress; and defining a problem in all its complexities is half of the way to solving it.

So how can the solutions be found?

Our study revealed that difficulties in communication are confounded by late referrals which lead to dementia being diagnosed later, thereby accentuating the problems of care by professionals. This means that at an input stage, work needs to focus on an information programme to stimulate awareness of the disease leading to earlier referrals by families and communities, as well as to encourage the take-up of services which are developed as 'appropriate'. We know that *no referrals* means *no assessment* means *no services*. Although we know that there is a relatively higher use of health services, including visiting GP's, by elderly Afro-Caribbean and Asians compared to white groups (Bhalla & Blakemore 1981; Ebrahim *et al.*, 1991), it is clear that the frequency of contact with GP's and hospitals does not necessarily reflect the quality of treatment received: *"I am not happy with my GP.....No one in the practice cares if you are a refugee and do not speak good English....I am a doctor myself, I knew I was suffering from malaria, but they didn't listen. They only said: don't worry it is cold weather, you come from a hot country, different food, culture"* etc. – a member in the survey of Primary Health Care for black and minority ethnic people – a consumer perspective (Fassil, 1996).

GP Issues

By contrast to the above alluded to survey, in a similar survey looking at GP perspectives conducted in two cities and one London borough with significant minority ethnic populations (Eccles and Kohli, 1996), the following comment was made: *"GP's often felt demoralised with the burden of frequent consultations (the heart sink scenario).....with little time to focus on chronic disease management"*. Regarding training, the survey was unequivocal in stating that *"professional education of GP's and especially GP Registrars should include ethnic minority culture and health problems...recognition of internal racism by Primary Health Care Team staff leading to negative attitudes towards certain groups. Prejudices need to be addressed"* (pgs., 8 and 18). The family GP is the first point of contact in accessing health and social services – and the pressures of this are all too apparent as expressed in the survey above regarding high consultations. This is exacerbated by social problems, including the 'letter syndrome' (*i.e. "can I have a letter for social services, housing?"*, etc.).

Our study and others (Brown, 1997, SSI Inspection; Donaldson-Carer Stress Project at Manchester University; NISW) all point to either a very low number of, or a complete absence of minority ethnic members with dementia in surveys of dementia care, despite the selection of areas which have an established minority presence. This has been attributed to a lack of members accessing health and social services. There is clearly a relationship between the absence/low rate of referrals of minority ethnic elders with dementia and the role of GP's – a role which *"GP's are not finding easy"*, even for people with dementia from the majority population (ADS, 1995). This corresponds to our point in the main Introduction regarding the lack of inclusion of minority ethnic groups in existing research projects on care methods and provisions (e.g. Ballard et al., 1994).

There are some 35,000 GP's in 11,500 practices in Britain (ADS, 1995; approximate figures) who have faced enormous changes following government changes to the National Health Service resulting from the NHS and Community Care Act 1990 (implemented in 1993). Although the impact of such demands over and above a GP's normal range of responsibilities and a lack of specialism in dementia need to be taken into account, the fact that a London survey of GP's (Graham, 1995 cited in ADS, pg. 15) found that "70% had great difficulty with the concept of dementia as a diagnosis and how to arrive at that diagnosis"...and expressed "that easier access to long term beds was needed and that the problem was mainly social" (Wolff et al., 1995, cited in ADS, pg. 15), suggests that there is a trend of neglect. In this regard, GP's are not aware of their power as 'gatekeepers' to other services in the process of making (or not making) referrals and, in consequence, are failing their minority and majority patients.

Cultural Training

In both our study and the survey cited above (Fassil et al., 1996), professional carers confirmed and recognised the need for appropriate 'cultural' training in improving their practice with clients. From Section 1 it is apparent that professionals were not asking for a 'checklist' approach to minority care. By 'checklist' approach we mean that questions are asked on how to respond to a minority ethnic person's care in their most simplistic form – e.g. placing stress on 'apparent' attributes such as food or dress. Such questions obviously need an answer. However a 'checklist' approach would suggest that such questions are sufficient and applicable to all who fall within the category of "X is a black service user and all black people therefore...". Moreover the approach suggests that the context of the client does not matter. Such an approach would, inevitably, lead to a narrow stereotypical picture of the preferences and needs of a minority ethnic client. It is also apparent from Figure 5 on 'solutions' put forward by professionals, that learning from other staff scores very low indeed. This may be because certain stereotypes develop and are passed on between staff. If professionals were to come up with a checklist based on such staff – staff learning, it would probably reinforce stereotypical/racist thinking and practice, which we termed 'stagnant thinking' in Section 1.

Our view would be that appropriate food and dress, ability to communicate, being able to exercise religious and spiritual practices in the maintenance of physical care are ordinary care considerations which we all take for granted. Considered from this point of view, asking for services which are culturally appropriate is not actually asking for 'special treatment'. The requirements are merely different. What do we mean by the 'context'? Discussion of ethnicity often omits the forces of racism and inter-group power relations, implying that multi-ethnic equality can be achieved with cultural adjustments (Sivanandan, 1991). For minority elderly with dementia, problems of racism, poverty, communication and inaccessible welfare services are intensified by their minority and/or migrant/refugee status. *A good practice approach which is sensitive to the needs of minority clients is to adopt an open-ended approach. Being receptive to situations rather than putting situations in a pre-designed framework is the good that we should strive for.*

Nevertheless, we can understand the attraction for 'checklists' as a solution to providing care for minority clients: with the current bombardment of internal pressures which public sector care personnel are experiencing, any 'new' element presented may be regarded as 'unworthy' of consideration or seen in its most simplistic form. In these circumstances clearly there is an appeal for a 'checklist' approach to care for people with dementia from minority ethnic backgrounds. It also ties in with the current trend in competence based training where the interpretation has resulted in a 'technocratic' approach by some.

Specialists and Competence

Finally, in order to meet the indicators of well-being in dementia cited earlier, a professional who is 'competent' in dementia care but omits the basic context of the demented person cannot attain the indicators as standards of dementia care. Similarly a professional who is 'competent' in ethnic relations but has no competence in dementia care cannot be expected to meet the standards of good care. In our study, professionals recommended the employment of specialist minority ethnic staff in dementia care. Specialist workers have emerged in many service areas in the UK, supported by the Race Relations Act 1976. They stimulate developments which may be non-existent, aid fellow workers and often act as the 'bridge' between the mainstream service providers and one or more minority community. The ADS has recently adopted this approach by recruiting one specialist ethnic minority staff member based in its regional office in Birmingham with a further possibility in its Newcastle Branch. However, questions clearly arise as to whether such an individual is there as a resource for an entire UK-wide organisation, or just for its regional office covering a large city with a significant minority ethnic elderly population. Leaving aside the built-in pressures of such appointments and how minority workers manage them (see Patel, 1995), our view would be to regard the recommendation of employing specialist minority ethnic workers as critical in stimulating care developments.

We also believe that health and social care providers need to seriously consider how dementia care to minorities is researched at a local level: there is an immediate need to feel that competence in dementia care is a sufficient criterion for recruiting staff. Inevitably, staff from the majority community frequently succeed in obtaining such posts. That is not a bad outcome since we believe in a multiracial workforce to reflect a multiracial society. However we do not see this outcome spreading evenly in reality. We would assert from practice that if such staff do not understand the complexity of ethnicity and the historical under-utilisation of welfare services amongst the minority elderly, then initiatives, albeit with good intentions, will remain ineffective. Rather, the answer lies in supporting minority ethnic workers to be competent in dementia care: this way resources from the community are built up and address the relationship between service developments and employment creation. These factors then take us to the heart of service developments, initiated and managed by minority ethnic organisations.

5. Minority Ethnic Organisations

The findings in Section 1 point clearly to the effective role played by minority ethnic organisations in managing the care of their members with dementia. With one exception, the residential and day care organisations we interviewed were providing services to all minority elderly. The exception was a voluntary organisation on Alzheimer's Care with a minority ethnic co-ordinator, operating in a part of inner London with a significant minority ethnic population. By virtue of their location and employment of minority staff, they were seen as having specialism not only in dementia but on minorities, and we therefore included them as part of our sample – although recognising that in theory they were a voluntary organisation catering for the entire mix of residents in the local area.

Approaches to Care – Reminiscence Work

We explained in Section 1 the range of approaches used (Fig. 1) and commented on the caution expressed by respondents. We briefly analyse here one aspect of care work - reminiscence.

Reminiscence is about re-collecting, remembering and re-connecting past experience, events and people. It helps to retain a sense of oneself and to remain in relationship with others. Reminiscence holds back the 'shrinkage' in people with dementia (Gibson, 1994). People like Professor Faith Gibson have made an enormous contribution to this method and its thinking in the mainstream, particularly in relation to group work. However, reminiscence work with minority ethnic older people, such as the examples we mention in our country profile, are not being recorded. The form in which reminiscence work is carried out is through photographs, storytelling, dance, drama, craft work, films and music. For example, in conversations we have heard how one can see the elders completely absorbed in songs and how they are able to reflect this joy in their body rhythm – age and dementia labels being cast aside. Music like other reminiscence tools clearly has the power to connect with Self. For one of the authors, an aunt who had severe dementia could recite perfectly several *Bhajans* (spiritual songs) in two languages 'with so much love expressed through the voice', but could not remember the family members – initially to their dismay and pain.

Our findings suggest that reminiscence work should be regarded as a useful tool for use with minority ethnic older persons with dementia. However, further work needs to be done to explore the effectiveness of the methods used including the effects of reminiscence and post-reminiscence on people with dementia. Within this we would want to explore the effect of cultural boundaries: by this we mean is the difference in the tools employed (appropriate language, music, drama *etc.*) and/or is the difference in the conceptual parameters created. These are important questions since there is the danger of merely inserting culturally appropriate reminiscence work aimed at different minority ethnic older people with dementia without critically examining the effects of age, social class and ideology in that culture. This danger of simple insertion was most visibly displayed at a significant Euro-Conference on reminiscence organised by the Age Exchange Theatre where two leading reminiscence thinkers in a discussion session answered to a question from the audience that the only *"culturally relevant factor in a mixed reminiscence group would be the issue of language"*. This and other views, experiences and issues merit serious and constructive consideration. The avenue for such considerations lies with the minority ethnic organisations and thinkers who specialise in this area of work. As we suggest later, it is necessary that the body of knowledge which needs to be built in this area along with human and social capital, come from *within* the minority ethnic organisations and personnel who actually work with minority ethnic older people suffering from dementia. This must in our view also require examination of mainstream research and practice developments to ascertain from where learning may be adapted. Perhaps some day in the true spirit of a real partnership, the mainstream will also learn and adapt from the practice developments and work with minorities suffering from dementia!

Barriers and solutions

The findings show that minority care organisations are facing several barriers, but are making efforts to overcome some of them (see Figs. 2 and 3). To understand the critical role played by such organisations we will begin by stating that *"in the absence of appropriate health and social service provision, such organisations have met minority elderly's needs"*. They have played a *substitute* role, essentially becoming the *primary* providers of care since there were no pre-existing provision of services to our target group. It is also recognised that such organisations have been financially supported and positively viewed by mainstream health and social services because they provide a 'buffer' against direct criticism of failure to provide services by the mainstream. Since they are characterised by small budgets, often on a short-term basis, with poor infra-structure, a 'fringe' provision is created which in a climate of financial stringency can be trimmed, cut or stopped, as shown by various authors (Patel, 1990; Atkin, 1996).

Given this structural context, and the rising numbers of minority elderly (see Part 1: The UK country profile), it is all the more remarkable that the organisations we interviewed were *actually* responding to the 'new' problems of minority elderly with dementia. In Section 1 we presented the barriers they identified, the difficulties they managed, the range of approaches with which they were familiar and the clear recommendations that they put forward as being necessary to improve care and in achieving the indicators of relative well-being for their members with dementia. From this, two clear conclusions emerge:

- there is scope and potential for minority ethnic organisations to be the major providers of care for minority ethnic elderly with dementia;

- policy makers and professionals must support such developments.

The capacity of minority ethnic organisations as 'specialists'

In the UK, the NHS and Community Care Act 1990 (implemented in 1993), with its market-oriented approach and unwillingness to recognise structural barriers to minority elderly, have threatened to exacerbate their situation within an increasingly chaotic and shrinking welfare society. Add the effects of stereotyping and gate-keeping considered under family and professional carers above, and we can begin to appreciate how effectively these work to keep minority elderly with dementia 'out of the market' – according to the market dynamic, if you cannot register demand for services, it follows that they *do not* have need for such a provision!

This is recognised in the forthcoming guidance from the Department of Health and the Department of the Environment 'Race, Culture and Community Care – an agenda for action in social services, health and housing' (1997). It states in its introduction:

> *"These deficiencies will only be overcome by a concerted effort from local and health authorities to agree joint action strategies, in partnership with the ethnic minority communities themselves.*
>
> *We recognise that progress will, in most areas, require:*
>
> - *challenging past attitudes, practices and assumptions;*
>
> - *redistributing resources in order to achieve equity;*
>
> - *impacting on every aspect of community care policy, planning, commissioning, providing and monitoring services;*
>
> - *revising management and employment practices.*
>
> *Making more resources available while operating under financial constraints is inevitably difficult - but will be the test of whether an agency is committed to the principle of equity of provision on the basis of assessed need, which is fundamental to the progressive shift from historical to needs - based patterns of expenditure (pg 10 -11).*

The explanation thus far confirms that the need for dementia care is there and the recommendations (see Figs. 3, 5 and 6 and Section 1) provide the 'ground' to be covered for our target group. Given the above context we are faced with an obvious solution to stimulate developments in dementia care. The solution lies in investing adequately and appropriately in the minority ethnic voluntary organisations, such as the ones we interviewed. As discussed above, this is because they are already in the 'market' providing appropriate care where none existed before (Norman 1985). Moreover, they are responding to a range of service needs including, from our perspective, dementia. This solution is quite a departure for one of us who prior to the community care changes, argued against 'separate service provision' in the belief that this reinforced marginalisation and offered a cost-effective response to mainstream providers (Patel, 1990).

6. Supporting minority ethnic organisations in specialising in dementia care: the Satellite model

The introduction of community care with its market oriented reforms has altered the balance: minority organisations have had to engage with the changes and enter into contracts or obtain grants as *providers* of care supplying services to meet the demands of purchasers. Interestingly, given the context of how services for minority elderly have developed, providers are having to furnish information to register demand with purchasers. Purchasers can then express demand to meet needs of local people, supplied by providers. All is not perfect in the 'market' of care!

To argue for better resourced minority organisations who can meet the care needs of people with dementia is not to suggest that such services become exclusive. On the contrary, a majority of the organisations we interviewed had members from mixed minority groups with different faiths, customs and languages. Their common element was belonging to a 'minority'. Nor did they exclude members from the majority population. Indeed at one weekend respite centre, the policy was for a multi-ethnic group to reflect the local population, and staffed by a mix of multi-ethnic workers. A Polish residential home we interviewed was exclusively Polish, though this was changing with 'mixed-marriages'. The reason for exclusivity here was entirely to do with a legislation after the Second World War where an accord was reached to 'look after the polish servicemen and women involved in the war effort'. A Jewish residential home was also beginning to open access to non-Jewish members.

In addition to better resourcing of minority organisations, we would propose a *'satellite model'* approach to respond adequately to the development of dementia care. A 'satellite approach' would be comprised of identifying a small number of minority organisations in key inner city areas whose task would be to generate specialist knowledge and developments in dementia care, encompassing the areas of recommendations considered fully in Section 1[2]. Like any new developments, the 'satellite' projects would need a structure and injection of investment. The aim is to clearly help meet the indicators of well-being in the person with dementia and act

- as stimuli (relevant information of the local market for purchasers) and

- resource providers to a range of minority organisations.

This would enable the development of comprehensive resources, education, methods, staffing and infrastructure to be clearly focused on one aspect of elderly care: dementia, which could be utilised by many. This would help address major problems of access, appropriate care and the low knowledge base on dementia among minority communities. In turn it would help to raise expectations of what care is possible, and where and how to obtain it.

To care or not to care....

The alternative to not pursuing development in targeted specialist organisations as proposed here, is to continue with *ad hoc* approaches with little information on issues, experiences or methods of care being shared – to the detriment of the person with dementia and their carer. Since dementia is considered to be on the margins in the eyes of wider society (ADS, 1995; Rasmussen, 1997), this places the issue of dementia amongst ethnic minorities within a sub-section of this marginalised area, suggesting that a different approach in care planning as suggested here for minority communities is urgently needed. Ironically this should be possible since the area of dementia is under attack from the *"competition for scarce resources in health, the struggle to balance budgets...and no one can escape the rules of the market"* (Rasmussen, 1997). Faced with this reality, the neglected area of minority elderly care in dementia exercises our minds to look at alternative models which can be effective *if allowed the opportunity for experimentation and the support of innovation*. It may even open up possibilities to transfer learning to the majority group in dementia care – and that would be a good test of 'equality' in knowledge and practice from the margins!

The responsibility lies with those managing the 'market for care'. If we regard management as *"an expression of human agency, the capacity actively to shape and direct world, rather than simply to react to it"* and argue that a *"manager deserves a morality"* (Hales, 1993, pg. 2), Weir (1997) continues, *"the good manger can never accept the world as it is, less justify it"* – then directed support needs to be given by relevant authorities (from government to the statutory, voluntary, and independent

---

[2] We are mindful of the fact that a list of approaches cited by respondents in dementia care as explained in Section 1 does not signify qualitative aspects of those very approaches. This aspect needs to be considered as part of development work which would be the result of 'satellite projects' development. Neverthless respondents must be aware of this aspect in order to express the range of recommendations one of which was training and specialist support.

sectors responsible for community care) in response to the findings expressed in our project so that they can be meaningfully implemented.

It is possible that we will recognise both the tree and its many branches if our findings are activated into proposals - these proposals would ultimately overturn the following sentiment shared by all respondents and Professor Mary Marshall,

" the world of dementia is colour-blind and minority communities are dementia-blind".

References

Alzheimer's Disease Society (1995) *Right from the Start – Primary health care and dementia, a report*, ADS

Askham, J. et al.(1995) *Social and Health Authority Services for Elderly People from Black and Minority Ethnic Communities,* London : HMSO

Atkin, K. (1996) 'An opportunity for change' in W. Ahmad and K. Atkin (eds.) *'Race' and Community Care,* Open University press.

Barnes, D. (1997) *Older People with Mental Health Problems Living Alone: Anybody's Priority?* Social Services Inspectorate, Department of Health

Bhalla, A. and Blakemore, K. (1981) *Elders of the Minority Ethnic Groups*, AFFOR

Blakemore, K. and Boneham, M. (1994) *Age, Race and Ethnicity*, Open University Press

Bohnstedt-M; Fox-PJ; Kohatsu-ND (1994). Correlates of Mini-Mental Status Examination scores among elderly demented patients: the influence of race-ethnicity. *J-Clin-Epidemiol.* **47(12)**: 1381-7.

Boneham, M. et al (1997) Elderly people from ethnic minorities in Liverpool: mental illness, unmet need and barriers to service use, *Health and Social Care in the Community 5(3), 173-180*

Bowling, A. and Farquhar, M. (1993) The Health and Well-being of Jewish People aged 65 to 85 years Living at Home in the East End of London, *Ageing and Society 13, 213-244.*

Brown, C. (1984) *Black and White: the third PSI Survey*, Heinemann

Brown, D. (1997) *At Home with Dementia: Inspection of Services for Older People with Dementia in the Community,* Social Services Inspectorate, Department of Health

Brownlie-J. (1991). *A hidden problem? Dementia amongst minority ethnic groups.* Dementia Services Development Centre. University of Stirling.

Carers (Recognition and Services) Act (1995) London: HMSO

CRE (1997) Race, Culture, and Community Care: Agenda for Action

Department of Health (1992) White Paper

Department of Health (1996) *Directory of Ethnic Minority Initiatives*

Ebrahim, S. et al (1991) Prevalence and severity of morbidity among Gujarati elders: a controlled comparison, Family Practice, 8: 57-62

Eccles, R and Kohli, B (1996) Primary Health Care for Black and Minority Ethnic People - a GP perspective *NHS Ethnic Health Unit Report*

Ethnicity in the Pharmacologic Treatment Process (1996). *Psychopharmacology Bulletin.* **32(2)**.

Fassil, J. (1996) Primary Health Care for Black and Minority Ethnic People – a consumer perspective *NHS Ethnic Health Unit Report*

Froggatt, A. and Moffitt, L. (1997) Spiritual needs and religious practice in dementia care in Marshall, M (ed.) *The state of art in dementia care*, Centre for Policy on Ageing

Graham, N. (1995) GPs and Voluntary Organisations in *ADS Report: Right from the Start*, op. cit.

Gray-A; Fenn-P (1994) The cost of Alzheimer's Disease in England. *Alzheimer's Review.* **4(2)**: 81-84.

Gibson, F. (1994) Reminiscence reviewed in Bornat, J.(ed.) *Reminiscence Reviewed*, Open University.

Hales, C. (1993) *Managing through Organisation,* London: Routledge

Hickman, M and Walter, B (1997) *Discrimination and the Irish Community in Britain*, London: Commission for Racial Equality

Kitwood, T. and Bredin, K. (1992) Towards a theory of dementia care: personhood and well-being, Ageing and Society 12: 269-287

Kitwood, T. (1997) *Dementia Reconsidered — the person comes first*, Open University

Lindesay, J. et al (1997) Knowledge, Uptake and Availability of Health and Social Services among Asian Gujarati and White Elderly Persons in *Ethnicity and Health, 2 (1/2): 59-69*

Lindesay, J. et al (forthcoming) The mini-mental state examination (MMSE) in an elderly immigrant Gujarati population, *UK International Journal of Geriatric Psychiatry*, vol. 12

Loewenstein-DA; Arguelles-T; Barker-WW; Duara-R (1993). A comparative analysis of neuropsychological test performance of Spanish-speaking and English-speaking patients with Alzheimer's disease. *J-Gerontol.* **48(3)**: 142-9.

Marshall, M. (1997) Introduction, in Marshall, M (ed.) *State of the art in dementia care*, Centre for Policy on Ageing

Mungas-D; Marshall-SC; Weldon-M; Haan-M; Reed-BR (1996). Age and education correction of Mini-Mental State Examination for English and Spanish-speaking elderly. *Neurology.* **46(3)**: 700-6.

Netto, G. (1996) *"No one asked me before"*, SEMRU and VOCAL

NHS and Community Care Act 1990, London : HMSO

NHS Ethnic Health Unit (1996) Directory 1995/1996 Health Care for Black and Minority Ethnic People.

Norman, A. (1985) *Triple Jeopardy: Growing old in a second homeland,* Centre for policy on Ageing

Owen, D. (1996) Size, structure and growth of the ethnic minority populations in Coleman, D and Salt, J. (eds) *Ethnicity in the Census*, vol.1 London: HMSO

Patel, N. (1990) *A 'Race' Against Time? Social Services Provision to Black Elders,* London: Runnymede Trust

Patel, N. (1993) Healthy margins: black elders' care — models, policies and prospects in W.I.U.Ahmad (ed.) *'Race' and Health in Contemporary Britain,* Open University Press

Patel, N. (1995) 'In search of the holy grail' in Hugman, R and Smith, D (eds) *Ethical Issues in Social Work London:* Routledge

Paykel-ES; Brayne-C; Huppert-FA; Gill-C; Barkley-C; Gehlhaar-E; Beardsall-L; Girling-DM; Pollitt-P; O'Connor-D (1994). Incidence of dementia in a population older than 75 years in the United Kingdom. *Arch-Gen-Psychiatry.* **51(4)**: 325-32.

Pharoah, C. (1995) *Primary Health Care for Elderly People from Black and Minority Ethnic Communities,* London: HMSO

Rasmussen, L. (1997) Conference paper delivered at the 13th International Conference: *the Blind Hunter,* Helsinki

Ratcliffe, P. (1996) Social geography and ethnicity in Ratcliffe, P. (ed.) *Ethnicity in the Census,* vol.3 London: HMSO

Richards-M (1996) Dementia in older African Caribbean migrants to the UK. *Alzheimer's Disease Society Newsletter,* Nov.

Rocca-WA; Hofman-A; Brayne-C; Breteler-MM; Clarke-M; Copeland-JR; Dartigues-JF; Engedal-K; Hagnell-O; Heeren-TJ; et-al (1991). Frequency and distribution of Alzheimer's disease in Europe: a collaborative study of 1980-1990 prevalence findings. The EURODEM-Prevalence Research Group. *Ann-Neurol.* **30(3)**: 381-90.

Sivanandan, A. (1991) 'Black struggles against racism' in Patel, N. et al (eds) *Setting the Context for Change No.1* Antiracist Social Work Education Series, Leeds: CCETSW

Smith, D. J. (1977) *Racial Disadvantage in Britain: the PEP Report,* Penguin

Social Services Inspectorate (1996) *Assessing Older People with Dementia Living in the Community: Practice Issues for Social and Health Services,* Department of Health

Tagore, R. (1915) *Songs of Kabir translated,* New York: Samuel Weiser

Warnes, T. (1996) The age structure and ageing of the ethnic groups in Coleman, D and Salt, J. (eds) *Ethnicity in the Census,* vol.1 London: HMSO

Weir, D. (1997) 'The ethical basis of management' in E.Marshall (ed.) *Business Ethics,(9705) Working Paper series,* Management Centre, Bradford University

Wolff, L. E et al (1995) Do General Practitioners and Old Age Psychiatrists differ in their attitude to dementia? in *ADS Report, Right from the Start* op.cit

74

1. Approaches in Care

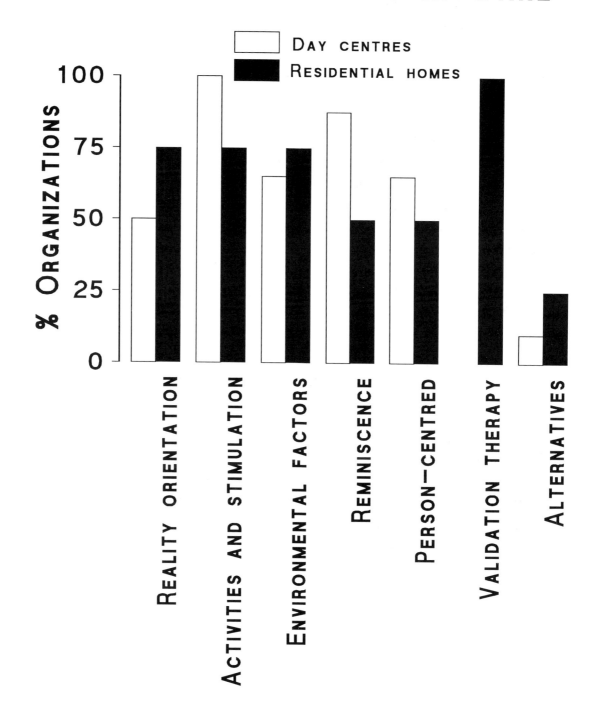

2. DIFFICULTIES ENCOUNTERED

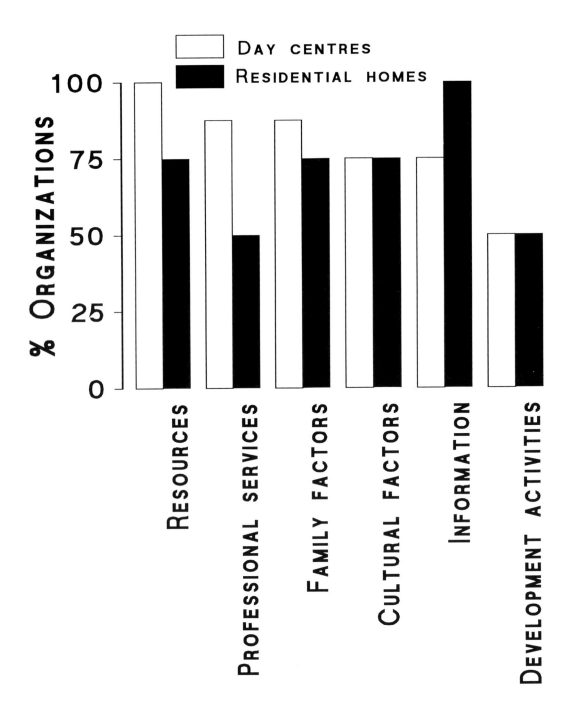

□ DAY CENTRES
■ RESIDENTIAL HOMES

% ORGANIZATIONS

100

75

50

25

0

RESOURCES

PROFESSIONAL SERVICES

FAMILY FACTORS

CULTURAL FACTORS

INFORMATION

DEVELOPMENT ACTIVITIES

3. SUPPORT NEEDED

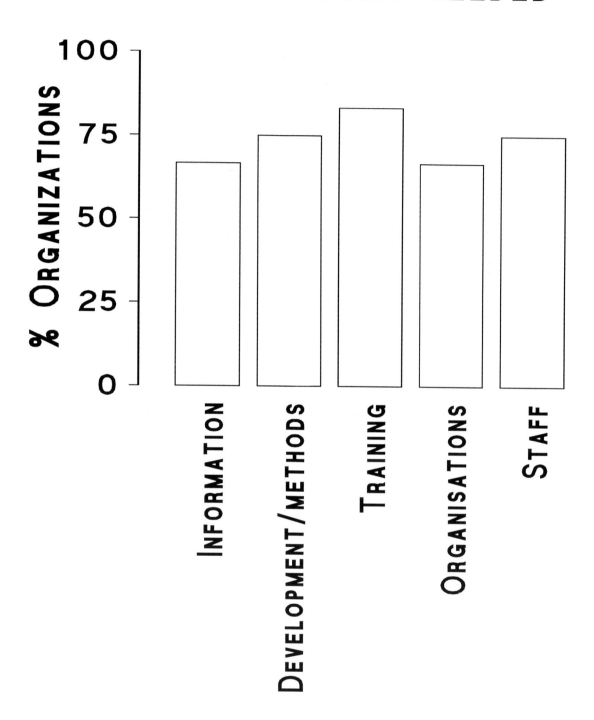

4. Issues related to EM patients

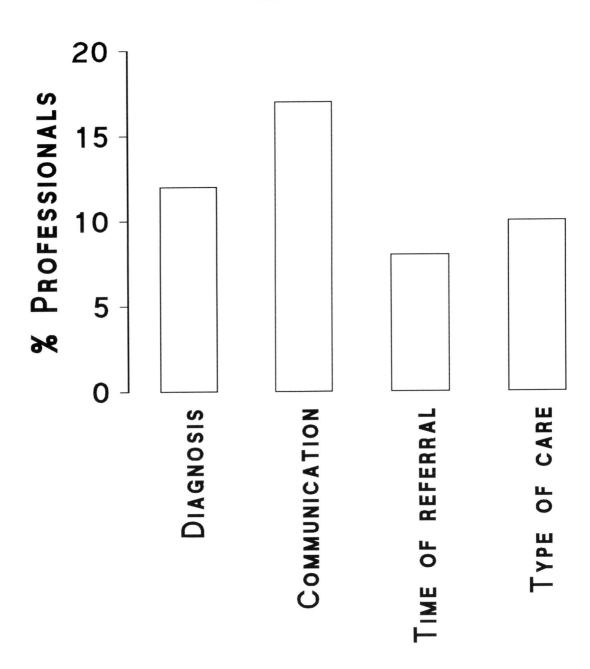

5. SOLUTIONS

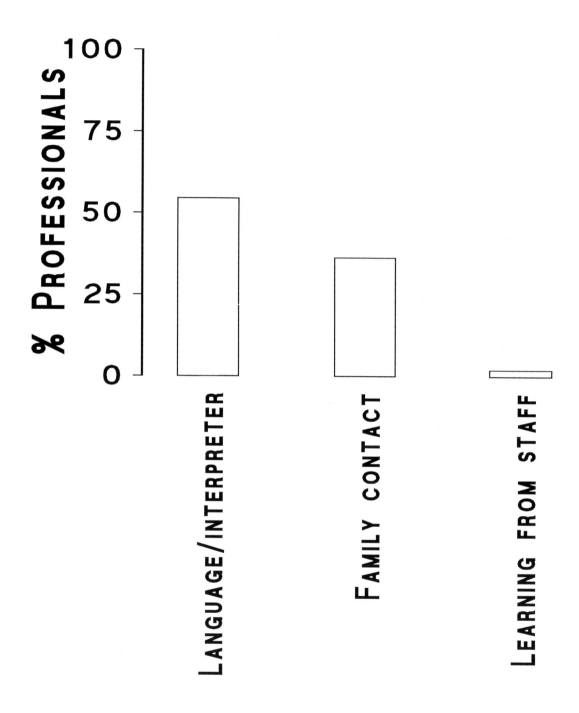

6. How to improve practice

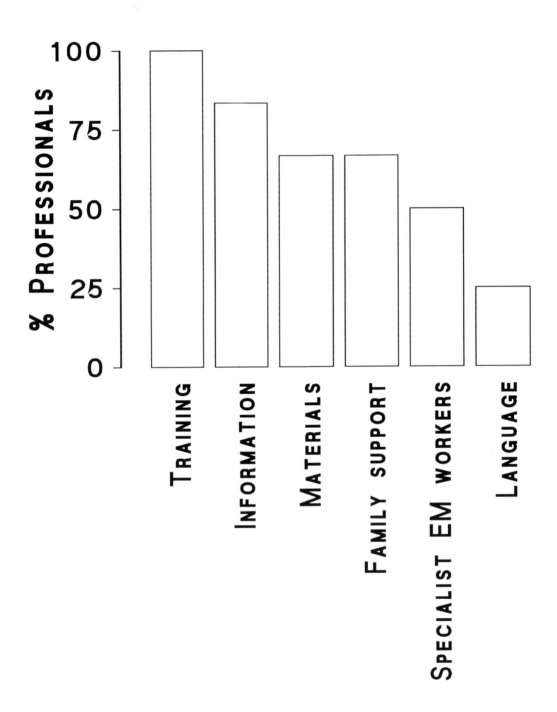

Denmark

Peter Lindblad and Kirsten Amstrup

Acknowledgements

We would like to express our appreciation to all the people who helped us during this project with information and comments. Special thanks for the help, criticism and feedback given to us in writing of the part, "the Good Practice Guide" from our colleagues at the Danish Institute of Gerontology and the CNEOPSA team.; especially recognition must be given to Christene E. Swane, Dorthe Høg, Susanne Palsig, Susanne Kagaard, Naheed Mirza, Bodil Johnsen, Sajida Afzal for their advice and support during the project.

Part 1: The Danish Profile

When speaking of older migrants there are a number of serious considerations regarding the concept of 'old'. For example, what does old mean? Is it possible that people who are old all belong to one group? Do older people share common norms, rules and behaviour? When are you old? Those working with older people are aware that old people do not have common norms, rules and behaviour – only numeracy defines age, but this is not the same as actual age. Older people are just as different from one another as young people and, although we are born the same, our life experiences make us different. It is not possible to speak of older people as one group; rather one should speak in terms of many groups in the same way as migrants are very different from one another. If we take Turkey, for example, we can see the cultural and ethnic diversity between a range of groups within the one country – ethnic Turks, Kurds and Tartars.

1. Pattern of migration to Denmark

Denmark has not been a major colonial power in the same way as Great Britain or France. Consequently, the pattern of migration differs from these countries. The only 'colonies' Denmark still has are Greenland and the Faeroe Islands.

At the start of this century, many Polish migrant workers were recruited for the sugar industry in Lolland. After the Second World War and at the start of the Cold War a number of political refugees arrived from Eastern Europe, many of whom were Jews. If a Danish politician was asked about these people s/he would probably answer, "these people have been assimilated into Danish society". However, if you ask in clubs for older Poles or Hungarians, for example, they will tell you that they have not been assimilated and feel they have been forgotten by society.

In the late 1960's and early 1970's the first guest workers from Yugoslavia and Turkey arrived in Denmark, having first worked or tried to find work in Germany and Sweden. Many of these people, primarily men, worked in Danish industries where there was a great demand for workers who were willing to take dirty and low paid jobs. Over the years, Denmark has also received refugees from Vietnam, Sri Lanka, Chile, Lebanon and other countries, and more recently from the former Yugoslavia.

2. Older migrants' situation in Denmark

Older migrants have particular concerns regarding the state pension. Many had expected to return to their own country with enough money to live in security and had not foreseen growing old in Denmark – consequently, many of these people may not qualify for the state pension. Not having planned on remaining in Denmark when old, few invested in property in Denmark or in private pension schemes. Therefore, their retirement income is wholly dependent on receiving a state pension, which must be qualified by residence in Denmark for 40 consecutive years. If these requirement are not met older migrants become dependent on state welfare.

Most older migrants have a common problem with language as they do not speak Danish very well. The language problem gives rise to many other problems. Thus, they do not receive information on activities for older people in day centres, and even if they were to go, they would not be able to communicate with anyone. Being unable to understand Danish television or radio poses a restriction on how they might learn about existing or new initiatives, or activities for older people. Furthermore, the language problem isolates older migrants from Danish-speaking older people, which may lead to prejudice and discrimination on the part of old Danish people.

The seriousness of the language problem is best illustrated in the context of older migrants' need to visit their physician, receive medical care in hospital or use domestic care services. A very important aspect of the Danish culture of care is based on activity, and old people are expected to participate in their care programme as much as they possibly can. However, this attitude is in conflict with many older migrants' ideas of growing old; as many frequently expect their children to play a large part in looking after them when they grow old. Like older migrants, the Danish government and municipal councils originally believed that migrants or refugees would return to their own country when old or, if they did not, that their children would take care of them. In neither case is this proving to meet with expectations.

Danish care and welfare policy and its implications for migrants and refugees

In Denmark, social and health policy is based on the principle of solidarity and the individual's needs are assessed accordingly. The role of the family, private voluntary organisations etc. is minimal. At the age of 67, one has the right to a state pension or social benefits. These benefits are equivalent to approximately 85% of an unskilled worker's wage, but many people are able to enhance their retirement income if they have had a trade union or private company pension scheme.

The Danish system is further characterised by the fact that, in relation to the needs of older people, all but a few services, such as specialists and hospitals, are taken care of by local authorities. Domestic services such as meals-on-wheels, community care, general practitioners (GPs) etc. are organised and financed by local authorities and paid for through local tax revenues.

The concept of care for older people is based on the premise of strengthening the possibility of older people leading independent lives in the community, but at the same time being able to access services should they be required. For example, domestic help/home care consists of cleaning, shopping, cooking, washing, personal care and treatment of wounds etc. Day centres are used by approximately 7% of the population over 60 years and the number of old peoples homes is decreasing and being replaced by service centres and sheltered housing.

Demography

There are 5,282,111 (1997) people in Denmark, of which 237,695 are from a minority ethnic group 0310 comprising 4.5% of the total population. In Denmark there are over one million people aged 60+ which makes up 19% of the total population.

People from the Danish "colonies" or rather the home rule areas represent 11,222 people from Greenland, of whom approximately 2000 are between 55 and 60+, and 10,385 persons from the Faeroe Islands, mostly young people living in "southern" Denmark (Denmark Statistics, 97). These people do not appear in statistics because they are supposed to be Danish and integrated into society.

Migratory patterns show concentrations in principal cities such as Aarhus, Odense, Copenhagen, and Aalborg, and in some areas of these cities concentrations can be as high as 40-50%. Two thirds of the minority population live in Greater Copenhagen and Sealand. To get an overview of the number of old people from minority groups in Denmark likely to experience problems with the care system due to differences in cultural background and language difficulties, one has to look at the statistics on persons born abroad living in Denmark.

Table 1: Persons born abroad living in Denmark

Origin	Age Group		
	50-59 year	60+year	Total (0-60+)
European	22.230	24.908	173.406
Africa	01.369	00.668	022.619
America	00.647	01.645	010.371
Americas	00.599	00.569	007.700
Asia	04.928	04.068	082.992
Oceania	00.077	00.095	001.864
Stateless	00.071	00.095	000.485
Total	29.921	32.027	299.437

(Denmark Statistics 97:6)

Table 2: Selected groups of elderly persons born abroad

Country	Age Group		
	50-59 year	60+year	Total (0-60+)
Germany	5.524	7.055	25.859

Norway	2.235	3.522	14.897
Sweden	2.288	2.950	17.905
UK	1.608	1.375	12.754
Turkey	2.258	1.265	26.353
Yugoslavia	2.520	2.011	27.609
Iran	0.473	0.519	10.339
Lebanon	0.374	0.336	11.520
Vietnam	0.383	0.793	07.676
Pakistan	1.252	0.435	08.877

(Denmark Statistics 97:6)

Main ethnic minority groups in Denmark

(I)   The Jews are the oldest and best organised minority group in Denmark. The Jews define themselves as one minority group although they only have their religion in common. It is not possible to get exact statistical information on this group. The reason for this is that elderly Jews come from all over Eastern Europe, and some have been living in Denmark for generations. The Jews have organised housing for elderly Jews, and two Jewish nursing homes exist. In one of these homes 80% of the people living there have an Eastern European mother tongue. However, they do not have Yiddish, Hebrew or Danish as a common language, and therefore comprise a heterogeneous group within themselves.

(ii)   The largest minority group in Denmark are Germans. Most live in the border area between Denmark and Germany, and it is customary that Germans get German-speaking help and institutions and Danish people get Danish-speaking help and institutions.

(iii)   Although there is a rather large group of elderly people from Norway and Sweden living in Denmark, no special elderly care exists for these groups since the Norwegians and Swedes are supposed to be integrated into Danish society because of a common cultural background.

(iv)   Refugees and migrants from the former Yugoslavia represent a new group of elderly people in Denmark. This group has been divided into small groups and live in various municipalities all over Denmark, and at present there is no special elder care for this group.

(v)   The Turkish group, or one should rather say the Kurdish, Tartar and ethnic Turkish groups have various kinds of 'day centres' and clubs for elderly people, but there is no official care policy towards this group.

(vi)   There is a rather large group of Asian elderly living in Denmark 0310 the Vietnamese, Pakistanis, Iranians and Lebanese comprising the larger elements. In the past some projects on elder care with these groups have been carried out, but only a few projects have turned into long term strategies. The statistics also show a group of elderly people, some of whom are Asians, from the UK, but it is likely that many carry UK passports.

Generally speaking, it could be said that the German minority group have no problems concerning "ethnic minority sensitive elder care or special dementia care". However, the other minority groups above, with the exception of the Jews, have no "ethnic minority sensitive elder care or special dementia care". Regarding the Jews it is important to realize that although they have their own institutions, many of these people do not speak a common language or the language of the staff. Furthermore, nearly all have a non-Jewish background.

3. Alzheimer's disease in Denmark

Epidemiological profile

Prevalence according to age

By the year 2000, 19,5 percent of the Danish population will be over 60, representing nearly one fifth of the population, and in 2030 nearly a quarter of the population will be 60+. Since AD increases in frequency as we get older, it will become a greater concern for society in general. Table 3 shows the trend toward greater prevalence of dementia as age increases. However, dementia is a heterogeneous disease and therefore Tables 4(a), 4(b) and 4(c), respectively, show the trend for the prevalence of Alzheimer's disease (AD), vascular dementia and other dementia's in different age groups in Denmark.

Table 3: Prevalence of dementia

Age (years)	Men	Women	Average
65-69	04,9 %	02,7 %	03,7 %
70-74	05,8 %	05,2 %	05,5 %
75-79	10,3 %	09,5 %	09,8 %
80-84	17,2 %	11,5 %	13,8 %
Total	08,0 %	06,5 %	07,1 %

Table 4(a): Alzheimer's disease

Age (years)	Men	Women	Average
65-69	01,2 %	01,7 %	01,4 %
70-74	02,7 %	03,6 %	03,2 %
75-79	06,3 %	08,3 %	07,5 %
80-84	13,7 %	09,3 %	11,0 %
Total	4,4 %	5,0 %	4,7 %

Table 4(b): Vascular dementia

Age (years)	Men	Women	Total
65-69	01,6 %	00,2 %	00,8%
70-74	01,3 %	01,4 %	01,4 %
75-79	02,0 %	00,9 %	01,4 %
80-84	02,9 %	01,7 %	02,2 %
Total	01,8 %	00,9 %	01,3 %

Table 4(c): Other dementia's

Age (years)	Men	Women	Total
65-69	02,1 %	00,8 %	01,4%
70-74	01,8 %	00,2 %	00,9 %
75-79	02,0 %	00,2 %	01,0 %
80-84	00,5 %	00,7 %	00,6 %
Total	01,8 %	00,7 %	01,1 %

(Acta Neurologica Scandinavia, 1997, 95.
by Kjeld Andersen et. al.)

Prevalence of Alzheimer's disease amongst ethnic minorities

No information on the prevalence of AD or dementia amongst ethnic minorities exists in Denmark, although our research suggests that there is a 'hidden problem'. Nevertheless, an estimate can be made, if we use the figures from Table 3 (prevalence of dementia), and the figures from Table 1 (persons born abroad living in Denmark). There were 32,027 people over 60 and approximately 1,500 elderly persons (60+) from Greenland and Faeroe Islands. If we assume a similar ratio of one in 20 as for the general population, there are an estimated 1,676 people from ethnic minority backgrounds suffering from dementia in Denmark.

The cost of Alzheimer and related diseases in Denmark

Table 5: Expenditure on moderate to severe Alzheimer's disease in Denmark (1995)

Service	Number of visits	Expenditure/year in DKr
Hospitalise in somatic hospital	001.210 demented	12.336.620.000
Hospitalise in psychiatry hospital	001.050 demented	1.073.100.000
diagnosing	000.879 demented	16.298.909
out- patient treatment	009.200 visit	9.660.000
Shunt operation	000.088 demented	4.291.056
Nursing home	016.286 demented	4.885.800.000
Housing for the elderly	001.440 demented	498.818.880
Home help (visit)	019.974 demented	1.401.136.152
Home nursing (visit)	019.974 demented	286.576.400
GP (visit)	683.721 visits	68.372.100
Total	**039.960 demented**	**9.480.673.497**
Estimated numbers (5%)	039.947 demented	
Difference	000.013 demented	

(Demens - En tikkende omkostningsbombe Sundhedsøkonomisk analyse af dementssygdomme kap.VI Bente Lauridsen Ege. Københavns Universitet, Økonomisk Institut 1996)

Research and print information

In Denmark, nothing has been done in the field of research in the area of elderly people from minority groups with dementia.

Organisations

There are no organisations who relate to any ethnic groups that are working with AD or mental health in aged/older people.

Surveys on mental health

There is no information on ethnic issues in dementia.

Part 2: Establishing Current Knowledge of Good Practice

Introduction

It is surprisingly difficult to find elderly persons from the ethnic minority groups who actually suffer from dementia. There are probably several reasons for this. Firstly, in Denmark, many elderly people from ethnic minorities are Swedes or Norwegians, and they are not considered "ethnic minorities" because they look like Danes and many speak a kind of Scandinavian that most Danes understand. Also, GPs and the specialists on dementia we have interviewed in connection with this project claim that they very rarely meet such clients in our nursing homes, and it is possible that they and the other professionals we have interviewed do not regard the Scandinavians or Germans as ethnic minorities. In other words, we have reason to believe that many cases of dementia amongst ethnic minorities have simply not been reported. Secondly, amongst persons usually considered ethnic minorities, as for instance Pakistanis, Turks, Yugoslavians, Arabians etc., few are 60+. Thus, the prevalence of dementia in this group is not manifest yet.

Another reason for the difficulties encountered may be that ethnic minority groups often have little knowledge or understanding of dementia. Studies show that ethnic minority groups often consider the symptoms of dementia as normal ageing (Ballard *et al.*, 1993). This point of view has also been confirmed in our interviews with professionals. Consequently, people from ethnic minority groups may not necessarily consult their GP when they have difficulty with memory for example. One psycho-geriatric specialist proposes: "patients from ethnic minority groups take contact their GP rather late in the process of dementia. This may be due to the fact that the family hides the patient from the surroundings, as the social consequences of having a demented person in the family are severe". However, it must also be considered that people from ethnic minority groups will often experience and present their symptoms in ways that are not understood by a Danish GP, in which case the GP will not refer the patient to a specialist for further examination.

In cases where the GP in spite of the above difficulties will start examining the patient to exclude or make a diagnosis of dementia, there are also difficulties – not least because diagnostic tests of peoples' mental state are culturally biased. This means that the tests are not necessarily sensitive to symptoms of dementia if the patient is from a different cultural background. Thus, the physicians interviewed in this project unanimously express scepticism regarding the validity of the available mental tests: "It is almost impossible to make a correct diagnosis. The greatest problem in differentiating between dementia and post-traumatic stress disorder. Moreover the

Mini Mental State Examination Test cannot be used to diagnose mental problems of people from ethnic minority groups and other tests are not available to GPs".

In order to be instrumental in the first steps to create a "good practice guide" within this area, we wished at the beginning of the project to create a comprehensive survey of the situation and thereafter to focus on the demented person. The latter referring to questions such as: How many persons from ethnic minorities went to see their GP with symptoms of dementia?, How do the GP and patient interact?, Was it possible to make the correct diagnosis, so that the elderly person received appropriate help through the system?

The second main task we set ourselves was to illustrate what kind of help an elderly ethnic person suffering from dementia could expect to receive from the Danish system of care for elderly people, and whether this help corresponded to the needs of the demented elderly person and his/her family. Are there cultural and language problems that cannot be dealt with by the normal Danish system for care of demented people? Furthermore, dementia progresses through a number of stages, and there are possibilities of help from various professional people within the field at each stage. Therefore, our findings and analysis are discussed with reference to the progressive stages of dementia (see below). Below is an overview of how we have divided our task into a number of interacting parts:

Theory and Methodology

Explaining the theory and method we have employed and the groups we have been in contact with.

Results

(i)   Here we describe our findings from the various groups of professional people we interviewed.

(ii)   As mentioned above, we present out findings considering the stages of dementia – from mild, via modest to severe dementia. We present the possibilities and limitations of the system for a demented person from an ethnic minority background – what would the course of events look like for an ethnic minority demented person? and, what would the possibilities be at different stages of the disease?

Based on our interview material and our knowledge within the area, we attempt to create a course of events which show the possibilities that are inherent in the Danish care system for elderly persons, and demonstrate that such possibilities do not exist for an elderly person from an ethnic minority background. With this purpose in mind, an imaginary person has been created who we believe presents the problem in an adequate and clear way.

Our definition of good care – is good care possible when the demented person's cultural context and language are not fully perceived? Based on the experience and knowledge we have in the area, i.e. our background in the Scandinavian tradition for care-taking of demented persons, good care is described with the aid of examples. Observations made by participation in nursing homes for elderly people and the interviews with various professional staff have been used to create an example of good care. With these examples, we wish to highlight how difficult it is for an elderly person from an ethnic minority group to receive good care when the basic cultural context and communication are not present.

Conclusion

We end with some ideas on the direction needed to better care for demented elderly people from ethnic minority groups, and how one should use ones efforts to change the state of things.

Theory And Methodology

1. Theory

We believe that the foundation of a "Good practice Guide" should be based on an understanding of what lies at the root of the different experiences and actions taking place in and around the demented person. Our theoretical point of departure as to accomplishing this task has therefore been Qualitative Gerontology, described in The New Language of Qualitative Method as, "Qualitative research is also distinguished by a commitment to studying social life in a process, as it unfolds" (Gubrium and Holstein, 1997, page 12) and in Qualitative Gerontology as, "Qualitative Gerontology is concerned with describing patterns of behaviour and processes of interaction, as well as revealing the meanings, values and intentionalities that pervade elderly people's experience or the experience of others in relation to old age. In addition, Qualitative Gerontology seeks to identify patterns that underlie the life worlds of individuals, social groups, and larger systems as they relate to old age" (Rowles and Shulamit, 1988, page 6).

To achieve our task we have used *qualitative interviews* (interviews in depth) supplemented with *observation by participation* (Keith *et al.*, 1994). This choice was based on the fact that we wished to obtain a picture of the importance that dementia and ethnicity have for the person his/herself and for the various persons that make contact with the demented person during the course of dementia. Qualitative interviews constitute a method of collecting facts employed in qualitative research. The purpose of the method is to obtain knowledge on what is meaningful for the interviewed person and on what importance different actions and experiences have had in the person's life (Fog, 1994; Kaufman, 1994). Qualitative interviews are a time consuming method as the actual "conversations" can take a long time and are often followed up by talks to clarify what was said. Observation by participation take place in "real time", and may therefore stretch over 24 hours or even years. In our case, the observations by participation took place for full days followed up by additional observations during specific periods.

2. Methodology

Geography and Demography

The geographical spread. Information was gathered from areas where there are large concentrations of ethnic minorities. Thus, most of our information is derived from Copenhagen and suburbs and some was collected from Aarhus, Odense and Aalborg (see country profile).

The ethnic spread. The groups which participated directly or indirectly, include Pakistanis, Poles, Estonians, Russians, Moroccans, Turks, Palestinians, Vietnamese, Chinese, Indians, Germans and Greenlanders. We included background material on Finns, Swedes, and Danes.

The interviewed groups

We chose to start with **GPs** because they are "gate keepers" to the rest of the health system. It was thought that through the work of GPs with ethnic minority groups, we would get a comprehensive view on how many ethnic people with dementia existed in the system. We were interested in the interaction between elderly demented people from ethnic groups and the GP, and how this interaction functioned with regard to a diagnosis of dementia. We found it essential to have the diagnosis aspect further illustrated, and therefore we approached **specialists in geriatrics** with extensive experience in diagnosing dementia.

The management of nursing homes gave us a good picture of how institutions and families work together and where barriers exist between an understanding of the norms, rules and behaviour of ethnic minorities and the Danish system of professional care.

Staff, including staff from domestic care who work with demented persons daily, are the closest to understanding the problems and the frustrations both within themselves, the demented person and the family. The same applies to the **family** who to an even greater extent experience the problems and the barriers within their own culture, as well as barriers that exist between their culture and the Danish care system.

Contact

Method of contact. We tried to establish contact with GPs through letters, personal inquiries during conferences and telephone calls. In order to establish contact with nurses, we advertised in the newspaper "The Nurse", explaining what the project was about and encouraged nurses to contact CNEOPSA. Nursing homes and their staff were contacted by telephone and by references from one nursing home to another. Staff involved in domestic care were contacted in a similar way. Finally, relatives of demented people were contacted via staff in the nursing homes or through other professionals.

General practitioners. We sent letters to approximately fifty GPs in the Copenhagen area, plus some to GPs in Funen and Jutland. The letter contained questions relating to whether they were inclined to talk to us about the question of elderly demented people from ethnic minority groups, and asked if they had ethnic minority patients with dementia.

Qualitative interviews with GPs took between 2 – 4 hours, and were followed-up by shorter discussions for clarification of certain points. The main topics were: (a) did they have contact with demented persons from ethnic minorities?; (b) the possibilities of erroneous diagnosis; (c) were available diagnostic tests adequate?; (d) the reaction of the family; (e) linguistic and cultural communication problems; (f) do families approach somebody with the problem or do they have little understanding of what is wrong?

The specialist in Geriatrics. Qualitative interviews and short telephone conversations to explain the matter with specialist in Geriatrics in Copenhagen, as well as telephone conversations with specialists in Geronto-psychiatrics from other parts of the country took place. We also contacted Dr. Med. Sirkka Liisa Ekman (Sweden) who among other things has specialised in the problems involved in diagnosing dementia in immigrants.

In these interviews the focus was: (a) problems concerning the cultural content in the MMSE-test and in other tests that are commonly used today in Geriatric wards; (b) problems of interpretation and understanding – the different cultural background and as a consequence thereof, the differences in the expressions of the patient and the interpretation by the specialist; (c) problems on what dementia is for family members and their conception of the disease.

The management at nursing homes. Five qualitative interviews and eighteen short telephone interviews were carried out during the survey with Managers of nursing homes. The main topics in the interviews were: (a) everyday life with a non-Danish resident; (b) food; (c) other residents; (d) staff; (e) co-operation with the family; (f) communication, mutual understanding and friction due to a different cultural context;

(g) possibilities of conflicts between the different cultures; (h) co-operation concerning death and funerals.

Superior visiting nurses. Four telephone interviews were conducted.

Care-taking staff, nurses. Five qualitative interviews, nine lesser interviews, and a number of short telephone interviews were carried out. During the survey with visiting and staff nurses, the interviews concentrated on the care conditions: (a) their view on the elderly demented from ethnic minorities; (b) special problems in care-taking; (c) how did they define "good care"; (d) co-operation with the family; (e) cultural traits that are difficult to understand; (f) the importance of the problems.

Relatives. Four qualitative interviews were carried out with relatives – it was not necessary to use an interpreter for this. The main purpose of the interviews was: (a) to illustrate how the family reacted when it was affected by dementia; (b) the social consequences to their own ethnic group in the case of care being entrusted to the Public Social System.

The demented person him/herself. We chose observations by participation in our approach to interviewing the demented persons owing to the considerable problems which exist in interviewing persons who are not only demented, but also have a different cultural background and language.

Analysis of qualitative interviews

Interviews typically lasted for 2-5 hours, and an interview guide was used. The guide changed during the course of interviews because our knowledge on the problems changed and also because problems differed amongst the different professional groups. We chose this form because it is our belief and experience that this reveals a good picture of the situation, especially regarding our target groups (Jackson, *et al.*, 1995; Gubrium *et al.*, 1994; Keith, 1994). We did not believe that such detailed information could be attained by other means – *e.g.* questionnaires and traditional quantitative enquiries. A few interviews were recorded on tape, although in most of the interviews notes were taken – this allowed us to return to the essential points in the conversation.

We shall, through a short exposition and discussion on our material from the different interviewed groups, give an account of the information we received. In order to illustrate our results with regard to Danish dementia care and the socio-cultural and linguistic problems facing ethnic minorities, we have created a little story. In this story, we introduce an imaginary **Peng** (made up on the basis of interviews with relatives, family and professional people in the field) suffering from dementia that progresses from mild to severe. The story allows us to simultaneously describe both the possibilities offered by the Danish social care system and the problems that exist for a demented person from an ethnic minority background. In a further example and for comparative purposes, we describe the story of *E* who is relatively well integrated into Danish society compared to **Peng**, but who through the stages of dementia loses the ability to speak Danish.

Analysis of observations by participation

The observations were accomplished in an "ethnic" nursing home over the period summer to autumn 1997. The observations were made by a nurse with 14 years of experience in working with dementia practically, theoretically as well as educationally. The results were discussed and analysed together with an anthropologist and part of the results were discussed with people with knowledge of dementia, at the Institute of Gerontology, Copenhagen.

Here we compare and describe "good care" in a Danish nursing home, with care in an "ethnic" nursing home. We illustrate problems with "good care" which can be explained as a result of differences in the cultural and linguistic context. We have again made use of stories of imaginary persons to illustrate the problems that exist, and also to maintain the anonymity of the persons involved in interviews. Ethnic minority people suffering from dementia are created on the basis of observations by participation, interviews and analysis carried out in the period spring to autumn 1997. The Danish person (*Emily*) who appears in the section on "good care" is created on the basis of the above-described Danish dementia care (see section above on Qualitative interviews), and adequately demonstrates "good care" for elderly demented persons in Denmark. Finally, in order to emphasise what "good care" is and to have "a method of measurement" we have employed Kitwood and Bredin's indicators (1992) throughout.

Results And Discussion

1. The Main Findings

Three major findings have been derived from our work. These we consider to be the essential results of this work:

- *Elderly demented persons from ethnic minority groups are to a high degree under- represented in the Danish Health System.*

- *Elderly demented persons from ethnic minority backgrounds encounter many barriers in the Danish Social and Health System, because they communicate their problems in a foreign language or in bad Danish and as a consequence of their different culture.*

- *Elderly demented persons from the ethnic minority groups who are gathered in "ethnic" nursing homes in Denmark suffer serious agonies and have many complicated symptoms in their state of dementia.*

In the following presentation and discussion of our results we would like to give an account of how we reached these conclusions. Furthermore, we would like to discuss how these conditions can be interpreted, and in conclusion we propose measures that could be implemented with a view to solving the problems that ethnic minority demented people encounter in Denmark.

2. Elderly demented persons from the ethnic minority groups in the Danish Health System

"Elderly demented persons from the ethnic minority groups are to a high degree under-represented in the Danish Health System".

As mentioned earlier we attempted to begin by ascertaining how demented people from ethnic minority groups seek out and receive care from the Danish Health System. However, although we sent approximately 50 letters to GPs we only received replies from two, both of whom informed us that they had not had contact with demented ethnic minority persons. Thereafter, we tried to establish contact with the GPs we had written to, via telephone. This direct approach succeeded in bringing about three qualitative interviews with GPs who did have contact with demented persons from an ethnic minority background in their practice. However, this approach contributed little to our understanding of ethnic minorities suffering from dementia. Consequently, we personally contacted by telephone a number of municipal domestic care arrangements and nursing homes in areas with large immigrant populations. We established contact with four departments of municipal domestic nursing. Two of these departments were situated in municipalities on the outskirts of Copenhagen and two of them in municipalities in North Sealand.[1] Our conversations with superior nurses who had the responsibility for extending domestic help and domestic care to the residents of these municipalities and who therefore had a comprehensive view of the clients that the municipal domestic help attended to, did not provide us with information about demented persons from ethnic minority groups. Only in one of the four areas was information forthcoming – in this case a family from Chile where a member was, in all probability, suffering from dementia.

Although, such a lack of information from GPs cannot unequivocally be interpreted as an expression of them having nothing to tell us, a picture started to emerge suggesting that demented persons from ethnic minorities only rarely received help from the Danish Health System, or that they were not visible as clients suffering from dementia – at least not as long as they lived in their own homes with their family. Either way it suggests that persons suffering from mild to moderate dementia from ethnic minority groups do not receive help, which the majority of them like Danes are entitled to.

To gain further insight into this issue we visited 18 different nursing homes and nursing centres, after having first interviewed the Managers of these institutions by telephone, where a large number of moderate to severely demented Danish people resided. Two of these nursing homes had an attached day centre for elderly persons and a number of protected accommodations, respectively. The nursing homes were situated in Copenhagen and surrounding municipalities and in North Sealand, *i.e.* in the same areas as the domestic care arrangements we had approached who were unable to tell us of any ethnic minority persons suffering from dementia, despite these being areas with large ethnic minority populations.[2]

Through the staff in these institutions, that in all accommodate over 2,700[3] clients, we got in touch with one (!) ethnic minority family amongst who one person made use of the day centre once a week because of a combination of dementia and problems in caring for him at home. In this day centre, situated in a densely built-up part of Copenhagen where 10,9% of the population are foreign citizen (Danmarks Statistik: Statistiske Efterretninger nr. 6, 1997) there had been in all only three different Asiatic men who had used the day centre within the last three years. Of these two men only one suffered from dementia. Subsequently, we established contact with a geriatrician specialised in dementia who was the professional medical consultant in the municipality and who gave advice to the staff in the nursing homes in Copenhagen in connection with residents suffering from dementia. This geriatrician had not met demented persons from the ethnic minority groups in any of the Danish nursing homes that she had attended to within the last few years.

After having inserted an article on our project in the Magazine for Nurses, a few people approached us, including two managers of nursing homes in Copenhagen who agreed to do qualitative interviews. Each of these nursing homes had experienced residents of non-Danish origin who suffered from dementia. In this way and through personal contacts we finally got to know about a few elderly persons of foreign origin suffering from dementia. However, it is clear that demented persons from an ethnic background are not often found in ordinary Danish nursing homes as well as having essentially no contact with GPs or municipal domestic care services. We may therefore presume that many of these people do not, even when they suffer from dementia, receive help from the Social and Health.

Summary

- The above results give no indication regarding to what extent elderly persons with dementia from ethnic minority groups approach their GPs in order to receive help.

- It is also surprising that among the relatively numerous domestic care arrangements and nursing homes that we had contact with, few had experienced caring for elderly persons from an ethnic background.

- It cannot be ruled out that the number of people from ethnic minorities who have reached the age where symptoms of dementia often occur (60+) are presently so small in Denmark that the group is generally not noted in the Social and Health System. However, it is also conceivable that this is a sizeable group in Denmark that, for one reason or another, does not seek or has not received help because they do not or are not considered to be suffering from dementia but instead from normal ageing. An absolutely certain conclusion on this matter will require a far more thorough study than what we have been able to accomplish within the time framework of the CNEOPSA-project.

However, two findings from our interviews suggest that ethnic minorities suffering from dementia are under-represented in the Danish Health System due to the latter of the two suggestions above – *i.e.* they are not considered to be suffering from dementia either by the family of the suffer or the system:

(I)   As we shall see, it appears from the interviews with both GPs and geriatric-specialists, that they have difficulty in identifying demented persons when the patient is from an ethnic minority background. This circumstance indicates that *diagnostic problems* are behind the absence of demented persons from an ethnic background in the Danish Social and Health Sector.

(ii)   Furthermore, we have found and have been in contact with a number of demented persons from well established 'ethnic' minority groups. The Jews are one of the oldest and the best organised minority groups in Denmark, in general a well-integrated and well-educated group with good social conditions and a good cultural network. This could indicate that a certain cohesion among ethnic minority families in their own cultural network constitutes a difficulty. This cohesion may explain the under-representation of these people in the Danish Social and Health system.

Notes:
(1)   Respectively 13,8%, 6,3%, 5,0% and 5,0% of the residents in the municipalities are foreign citizens. Source: Statistiske efterretninger nr. 6, Danmarks Statistik 1997. To these figures should be added an unknown number of elderly persons from an ethnic background who have obtained Danish citizenship.

(2)   We would like to draw attention to the fact that the persons we have been in contact with as most other Danes first and foremost think of people with a dark skin when one asks questions about ethnic minority groups. We had to ask directly if they knew about elderly persons from for example other European or Scandinavian countries and explain that these people were also part of the ethnic minority groups, in order to obtain knowledge about these groups. As will appear from the summary of the paragraph on

interviews, we got to know about a German woman in this way who suffered from dementia and established contact with her family.

(3)   The figures are based on an addition of the figures given by the managers we interviewed by telephone.

3. Stories and Interviews

"Elderly demented persons from ethnic minority backgrounds encounter many barriers in the Danish Social and Health System, because they communicate their problems in a foreign language or in bad Danish and as a consequence of their different culture.."

The story of Peng: mainstream dementia care in Denmark and the needs and possibilities for support for ethnic minority groups

Although there is a lot of information and discussion on the subject of Alzheimer's and related diseases in Denmark, studies show that it still takes a Danish family a long time to recognise that a family member is demented (Kirk & Swane, 1994, Ulla Isaksson, 1995, Mace & Rabins, 1987). From our talks with GPs, nurses, family members *etc.*, it is apparent that this problem is exacerbated amongst ethnic minorities, where the taboo of a family member suffering from dementia is greater than among the mainstream. However, it is very difficult to measure how big or small a taboo is from these talks.

To illustrate the problem and to simultaneously detail what mainstream dementia care in Denmark is (Formidlingscenter Nord, 1996; Gotfredsen, 1994; Swane, 1991; 1993), we will create a fictitious person from an ethnic minority background called **Peng**, based upon our interviews with professionals, carers and families. Furthermore, we will illustrate the "progress" of Peng through the different stages of dementia (mild, moderate and severe), and detail what contact Peng and his family have with the Danish Social and Health System and the degree of support they receive.

(i) Mild dementia

Dementia can develop over many years with different clinical manifestations at the various stages. Consequently the support that the demented person and his/her relatives require will differ throughout the phases of the disease. Early symptoms include memory problems, orientation, difficulty concentrating and, possibly, problems in formulating oneself (Amstrup, *et al.*, 1987; Gullmann, 1991; Swane and Kirk, 1994; Swane 1996). Even so, symptoms will vary from person to person, and therefore it is difficult to formulate standard care.

The story of Peng.....

Peng and his wife lived in an apartment located close to where their eldest daughter lived. The family were satisfied with this because when Peng's wife was ill and needed help with daily tasks, her daughter could give a hand. However, Peng started behaving strangely, although the family could not pinpoint anything specifically. His wife could not cope with looking after him and the home and so the family decided that Peng and his wife should move to their eldest son's house where they could live together more easily.

Peng and the general practitioner. When the family took Peng to the GP, the physician listened to the family's comments and did a physical examination and took blood samples to exclude any non-cerebral/somatic reasons for Peng's strange behaviour. However, the physician consulted with different members of the family as intermediaries and interpreter's and had great difficulty in getting a clear picture of the problem. Although on one occasion consultation with a professional interpreter was arranged, this did not clarify anything. Nevertheless, in the light of the families comments and Peng's age, the physician suspected Peng was in the early stages of dementia and briefly considered sending him to a geriatric ward for closer examination. However, he quickly abandoned this idea because of cultural and linguistic barriers. As one GP told us "there are a lot of communication problems – it is difficult to recognise the symptoms because the GP has a different cultural context". The family consulted other physicians without obtaining a solution to their problems. They had no idea that it was a matter of dementia.

Mainstream. The GP would listen to the patient and the patient to make an initial assessment, which in itself may indicate signs of dementia. In addition the GP will check for somatic or non-cerebral diseases which may explain the patients change of behaviour by physical examination and blood tests. However, if these do not explain the change in behaviour then the GP can tell the family that he suspects dementia or depression – this did not happen in Peng's case. To firmly establish diagnosis it would then be necessary for the patient to undergo a neurological and a neuro-psychological examination and/or be examined by a Geriatrician or by a Psychologist with experience in diagnosing dementia. In every day life, this is only done in very few cases.

Summary. It is apparent from the comparison above that GPs have great difficulty in understanding the patient and family, and therefore have difficulty in making a diagnosis. Moreover, families from ethnic minorities have difficulty in understanding the GP and the Danish Health and Social System (Lindblad & Mølgaard, 1993;1995). Furthermore, the cultural context needs to be considered since (i) the GP may not recognise the presented symptoms as indicative of dementia since migrants may convey the signs of illness differently, and (ii) some ethnic minority groups do not recognise the symptoms as dementia, but as "normal" ageing – what is dementia and how does the disease affect the every day life of the demented person and the family? (Kratiuk-Wall *et al.*, 1997).

(ii) Moderate dementia

The term "moderate dementia" is used in Denmark when some years have passed since the first symptoms were registered. Mild dementia symptoms worsen, the patient's ability to express him/herself linguistically will generally be diminished and often apraxia (difficulties in executing and co-ordinating ones movements) and agnosia (reduced ability to identify previously well-known objects) will become manifest (Amstrup *et al.*, 1987, Gullmann, 1991, Kirk & Swane, 1994, Swane, 1996). Thus the patient now needs more help to cope with everyday life.

The story of Peng.....

After a couple of years in the condition described above, Peng's state worsened. He argued with his wife and made lewd insinuations toward female members of the family. He could not be left alone without becoming unhappy and he could no longer wash, dress/undress or go to the toilet himself. Eventually, the burden on the family was too much and they repeatedly called the GP. The physician saw no alternative but to hospitalise Peng, who thus became a frequent "guest" in the hospital. However, in the hospital no attempt was made at trying to determine what was wrong with Peng – he was merely sent home again after a short stay without contacting the Social Help System.

Peng and the Social Help Apparatus. Even if Peng and his family had managed to enter the system, there might have been difficulties. As one professional caregiver told us: "I feel powerless in connection with the care of these people. I do not understand them and their 'world'. Communication is very difficult ...."

Mainstream. At this stage of dementia the following examples of practical help and relief to demented patients and their relatives can often be implemented by the GP or hospital (when the patient is discharged).

(a)   Need for practical support – domestic care and visiting nurse. When a Danish demented person reaches this stage of the illness, he/she will usually get help daily, e.g. ensuring that the patient has sufficient food, getting in/out of bed, taking a bath and sometimes help with administration of medicine. Furthermore, it is possible to get help for house cleaning and washing clothes.

(b)   Need for social contact – day care centres and day homes. Most Danish municipalities have centres for the elderly, which are commonly used by the "more healthy elderly" for social interaction and various activities. It is also possible that the elderly with serious health problems can spend a few days in the week either in day centres or day homes, again for social interaction and activities. These institutions cater for people in the early stages of dementia as well as non-demented people. In some municipalities, there are day centres, day homes, and respite care in nursing homes and elderly care centres, exclusively for people suffering from dementia. These homes/centres offer *stimulation* to the patient and at the same time provides *relief for the spouse* – hence allowing the spouse to interact socially, enjoy hobbies and other interests and get some rest.

Summary. In the case of ethnic minorities the practical help described above is unlikely to be extended or attained because the patient may not be diagnosed (or incorrectly diagnosed), and the patient and family are unable to explain to the GP or hospital the state of the patient and how this affects everyday life for the family. Even where a diagnosis of dementia has been established it may not be possible to get the right care because of the language barrier and the different cultural context.

(iii) Severe dementia

When the term "severe dementia" is used, the demented person is usually so handicapped by the illness that he/she will need constant help. Often it would be reckless or at least very disquieting for the family to leave the demented person alone, even for a short while. At this stage a Danish person with dementia who is living alone would probably already have been moved into an institution during the last phases of moderate dementia, whereas a demented person who has been taken care of by his/her spouse would move into a institution when they become severely demented.

The story of Peng.....

Peng's condition worsened – he started urinating in corners and started eating cigarette-ends. The family could certainly not cope with this and Peng was hospitalised again – this time the family did not want him to come back home and this led to a crisis between the geriatric ward and Peng's family. To solve the crisis the family explained to the hospital the extent of the problems they were now having with Peng. Only at this stage was it suggested that Peng could be suffering from dementia. A diagnosis of dementia was made, but only with difficulty. The people involved in the diagnosis said that they found it difficult to work through an interpreter in connection with the tests and conversations that are necessary to determine whether a person is demented or not.

Peng and the Danish day and night institutions

The story of Peng.....

After a period in the geriatric ward, Peng obtained a place in an ordinary municipal nursing home. The nursing home was not specially adapted with a view to taking care of elderly persons from ethnic minorities, but they were good at taking care of demented persons. Peng had a hard time at the nursing home during the first months, but over time he thrived. He established a good relationship with his contact person and with other elderly people in the home. In spite of the these good relations, there were problems at times. The staff felt something was missing in communicating with Peng due to the language barrier. As a carer said: "It was extremely difficult to experience him trying to tell something that he really wanted to express, and not being able to understand him". The staff had learnt important phrases such as "good-morning", but particularly during Peng's first year at the nursing home they were sure that Peng could have had more pleasure/stimulation through conversation. Indeed, at one stage the nursing home had an interpreter at their disposal and the staff were made aware of Peng's linguistic abilities. Overall, the staff at the nursing home were of the opinion that Peng reacted positively to the dementia care and treatment he received but that work with Peng was difficult because they did not have a common language and because the staff had no knowledge of Peng's background.

Mainstream. Today most Danish municipalities can offer living quarters in institutions fit for the individual demented person. There are small housing communities (group homes) in which 6-10 demented persons live together in a flat or a house, with staff present 24 hours a day. In many nursing homes some sheltered units for demented people are organised. Most of these are for 6-10 demented persons and they have good staff norms (Swane *et al.*, 1991; Swane, 1993). In most of these smaller units it is considered important to establish a sort of ordinary everyday life feel for the demented persons – for example, they carry out daily living tasks such as shopping, cooking, washing and cleaning. In some places gardening, taking care of domestic animals and activities around the coffee table are also encouraged. In other words, these small units are organised around a normal day, the content of which we call "miljøterapi" (environmental therapy). However, the term "miljøterapi" does not only cover practical activities. More importantly it involves tolerance, mutual understanding, acceptance and maybe affection or even love among the demented persons living together in these small units, and between the demented persons and staff members. It is equally important that there is enough "psychological space" in the unit to make room for the inevitable conflicts between residents living in such close proximity. The staff have to be qualified to help residents handle such conflicts. (Amstrup *et al.*, 1987; Swane, 1996).

In Denmark, one also finds demented people living in ordinary units in nursing homes. Such units were planned for persons with physical, not mental problems. Today more than half of the residents in these nursing homes are demented. It is common that the residents have their own "apartment". The apartment is arranged in co-operation with the family such that objects and furniture from the elderly person's own home reflect the environment that the elderly person came from.

Summary. In a well functioning nursing home for demented people from a Danish background the management will have taken the following factors into consideration (Swane, 1993).

- Selection and education of staff.

- Attitudes and atmosphere (psychological environment).

- Togetherness with other people (social environment).

- The physical environment.

- The structure of the daily life.

However, they do not take into account that a non-Danish ethnic minority person suffering from dementia may live in one of these homes. Thus, the selection of staff on this basis would have helped considerably in communicating with Peng, for example. Furthermore, staff are not educated on the subject of people from ethnic minorities and their special needs. Also, the environment and structure of the daily living routine reflect Danish norms, rules and behaviour.

However, the Danish experience does suggest that it is possible to create a good everyday life for demented people and their relatives, provided that you involve the relatives as associates, are aware that the demented person first and foremost is closely related to them (Kähler, 1996), and that there is a careful approach to the following factors: selection and education of staff, attitudes and atmosphere (psychological environment), the physical environment and the structure of daily life (Swane 1991; 1993).

The interviews

<u>General practitioners</u>. From fifty letters we sent to GPs in Copenhagen, Funen and Jutland we only received two replies saying they did not have any ethnic minorities with dementia. By making telephone calls and via direct approaches, we succeeded in completing three qualitative interviews with GPs who had an ethnic minority dementia patient on their register. Below we give a selection of the types of statements that these GPs made – the statements are given under the main topics in the interview.

(i) The problems involved in recognising a demented person from ethnic minorities

- When dementia is suspected, it is not because a person approaches somebody and explains: "I am suffering from dementia. People express concerns about memory problems or the family enquires about problematic behaviour in a member of the family".

- The family can bring along an elderly person and say he/she is demented but it is the physician's task to consider the problem together with the patient. ".... I do not deny that in most cases there are good reasons for the family to approach a physician, but family members can sometimes have their own particular idea about why mother or father is demented – we could use her house, now it is about time to entrust the old one to a nursing home, and so on..."

- If the person is known and has been followed through many years, changes in the patient that could draw attention to dementia, might be noticed: "Sometimes one could suspect that something is wrong if the patient has problems in taking his/her medicine ... small declines in personal hygiene ... there are small things that they do not understand that before never posed any problems ... the person in question has problems with the diurnal rhythm ... or the person always complains about the same things although there is nothing wrong ... it is difficult to say what exactly it is". The small hints can in most cases only be perceived in a common cultural background. Therefore, it is difficult for the GP to make his/her clinical eye function in relation to patients who have a different cultural and linguistic context.

(ii) *The possibilities of an erroneous diagnosis.* There are generally many reasons of an erroneous diagnosis of an ethnic minority person with dementia. One major reason is that the patient and the GP do not have the same perception, conception and context of the disease.

- "Problems of communication – even though an interpreter is used – can be so big that many consultations are needed to understand even minor problems ... sometimes it is not a matter of somatic problems, but more problems of personal character".

- "Dementia in an elderly patient from ethnic minority groups is not what I look for in the first place ... but with the amount of refugees from former Yugoslavia .. a syndrome of post-traumatic stress .. is a factor one cannot disregard'.

(iii) *Can the available diagnostic means be used?*

- "The diagnostic means (for example various kinds of tests) that are available are neither intended to 'catch' persons with a different cultural background, nor are they suited for another language ... even less intended to be used through an interpreter ...".

(iv) *The reaction of the family.*

- "Well, I have not had many of these cases, but sometimes the family has difficulties in understanding what has happened to their family member ... the family could have known for a long time that something was amiss but it can be difficult to accept that for example the head of the family suffers from dementiä.

(v) *Linguistic and cultural communication problems.* The general communication problem between the patient and the GP have already been mentioned. We were interested in the extent to which GPs believed that families actually approached them with the problem of dementia or whether they thought that the family did not understand what was wrong.

- GPs said that families did not approach them with symptoms of dementia, but rather with a number of other small problems. Also ethnic minorities registered with them had very little knowledge of the various forms of dementia.

- "I have never experienced a family that has approached me with the question whether their father or mother was suffering from dementia or not .. On the other hand I have been confronted with a number of strange symptoms of all imaginable things that finally suggests either depression, post-traumatic stress syndrome or dementia".

- "It can be extremely difficult to explain to the closest relatives that their mother suffers from dementia, the family's attitude is often that it is a matter of natural ageing or a punishment".

Summary. After having analysed our interviews with the GPs, we believe that the following are the main problem areas for ethnic minorities suffering from dementia and their families:

- Linguistic barriers.

- Culture specific problems – the social consequences.

- Differences in the perception of the disease.

- The family lacking knowledge of the disease.

- Slender possibilities of a correct diagnosis.

Specialists in Geriatrics

(i) The cultural specific content of dementia tests

- Is it possible to make a diagnosis when one does not speak the same language neither verbally or non-verbally? The specialist in Geriatrics said there were language problems in the use of the MMSE test: "I myself had to retranslate some parts of the test from American to Danish, as it otherwise would have given a completely erroneous – there is always a general problem in employing tests made in one cultural context to another cultural context".

(ii) Regarding interpretation and understanding

- "yes – it is possible to test a person from ethnic minorities for dementia ... but it can never be the same, when one does not have a common language ... there will always be a possibility of sources of errors in the translation one receives from the interpreter".

(iii) Different cultural backgrounds and consequently different expressions, interpretations and conceptions of dementia

- "We have had several cases where we made the diagnosis but the family did not understand what is was all about ... they took the elderly person home and tried with other specialists ... in this way we have had the same elderly person many times through the ward". This problem is confirmed in the only Scandinavian scientific report on 'Monolingual and bilingual communications between patients with dementia diseases and their caregivers', in which it was stated - "due to the fact that there has been intensive research into dementia in both countries (Sweden and Finland) valid tests were available in both languages. When (Finnish immigrants were) tested regarding cognitive and emotional functions by Finnish speaking researchers using Finnish instruments, it turned out that the persons studied did not appear as demented as they were considered to be by their Swedish-speaking physicians. A correct differential diagnosis is a necessary basis for optimal care. .... In fact it seemed likely that there were demented persons who had been placed in care facilities that did not meet their need for care adequately". (p.81)

Summary. With regard to the issue of diagnosing elderly ethnic minority persons as suffering from dementia, we would like to draw attention to the following:

- To sum up the situation on diagnostic problems: (a) it is possible to take blood samples; (b) it is possible to take a brain scan.

- Regarding diagnostic uncertainty due to language barriers and problems concerning the use of interpreter. It is not possible to make a correct diagnosis based on additional neuro-psychological tests if the physician does not speak the same language and does not know anything about the patient's cultural context.

The Management of nursing homes – everyday life with a resident who is not of Danish origin. The persons interviewed felt a certain frustration as to not having proper information on the cultural background of elderly persons. Problems could arise that were extremely difficult to solve as communication were difficult not only because of the dementia itself, but nearly impossible because of the difference in language. On the whole, they believed that ethnic residents could, without difficulties, be part of the activities offered by the nursing home.

(i) The food – in the ethnic nursing homes, attention had naturally been given to the food. But in Danish nursing homes where there are few ethnic minorities no special adjustment to their food needs had been made

(ii) The other residents

- "There can at times be problems with 'racism' in relation to other residents" – both on behalf of the Danish relatives and on behalf of the ethnic persons and their families.

(iii) The staff. The impression we got through the interviews with management was that the staff, generally speaking, did not believe that there were problems with elderly persons from ethnic minorities. However, they did say their were at times communication problems on a cultural and linguistic level.

(iv) Co-operation with the family

- "The co-operation with the family depends on what kind of a family it is, *i.e.* where they come from, what education they have, how long they have been in Denmark and how the 'chemistry' functions between the nursing home and the family".

(v) Communication, mutual understanding, and friction due to different cultural contexts

- "It can be quite difficult in the cases where an interpreter is needed or where the cultural differences are so big that we are not able to meet half-way".

(vi) Possibilities of clashes between the different cultures. There are many possibilities of clashes as regards different conceptions of how care should be given to an elderly person from an ethnic minority. What was stressed in our interviews in this regard were possibilities of clashes around the issues of activity versus non-activity and food.

- "It can be difficult to explain to the family that all the food they give the client, added to what he/she has been already served in the nursing home, might harm him/her".

(vii) Co-operation regarding death and funerals. It can be difficult for the management of the nursing home to co-operate with the family regarding death. Here the managers express their view that the cultural differences and their lack of knowledge of the client's socio-cultural context made it difficult for them to assist in making sure the death and funeral proceed well for all concerned.

Summary. Statements made by the managers of nursing homes can be summarised in the following points:

- Lacking knowledge of the person and the person's culture.
- Mutual racism between residents and relatives.
- Problems regarding food and rituals.
- Problems of communication.

<u>Care-taking staff (nurses).</u> Four qualitative interviews and a large number of short interviews by telephone, were carried out with care-taking staff. The interviews focused on the conditions of care and the perception of elderly ethnic minorities with dementia. There were no members among the staff we talked to that expressed a racist point of view directly. Their point of view was primarily that

- "the person is an elderly demented human being and that it should be possible through 'good care-taking' to see to their needs".

(i) Special problems in care-taking. Overall staff did not see any problems in care-taking. They tried to make the daily tasks function by learning short sentences and words in the patient's language. They felt that they could to a great extent communicate emotionally with the patient

- "I could see on her that she was happy, she smiled and patted my hand".

(ii) What did they perceive as good care. Staff we talked to have all worked for many years with demented persons and have therefore gone through various kinds of training within dementia care. They all agreed that it was the human being, the person in care that was essential and not the execution of daily tasks. This attitude could though, in everyday life, sometimes not be applied and then the task was given more priority than the person's feelings and his/her view.

(iii) Co-operation with the family. In the cases where the co-operation between the family and the contact person worked out well, it was a matter of 'good chemistry' between the two. In the cases we heard about, the family and the contact person always had a common language. It was possible to overcome cultural barriers with a combination of 'good chemistry' and an ability to speak the same language as the patient. However, in cases where the family and the contact person did not have a common language there were often serious problems in co-operating.

(iv) Cultural traits that are difficult to understand. Staff stated that on some occasions, the residents did some strange things that they put down to the cultural background of the person in question. It could be difficult to deal with such situations and help the residents to get on.

- "Once we had an Asiatic resident who meditated .. the first couple of times when he was laying in bed with a slow pulse, we called the doctor, but later we learnt that .. it did not mean anything ... he was always very happy when the meditation was over".

(v) The importance of the problems. Staff did not believe that it was a problem to have demented ethnic minorities in an ordinary nursing home. For them, the person was first and foremost suffering from dementia. Therefore, they believed that their

good care could compensate for the cultural and communication problems that may arise in the care-taking of the demented person.

Summary. The problem areas that the staff in our interviews and conversations pointed out were:

- Communication problems.

- Incomprehensible behaviour.

- The good care.

The demented person him/herself. Results on the observations by participation method below will consider this aspect with reference to stories such as that of Irina.

Relatives. It has been difficult to find families willing to take part in our survey to illustrate their reactions to dementia. We found it impossible to make a general statement from the interviews made, but there are some comments that can be made.

Ethnic minority families that have a poor background in terms of education and are deeply rooted in their traditional cultural pattern and view of the world, find it very difficult to accept dementia as a disease. If, for example, the oldest male person in a traditionally Muslim family is affected by dementia, this has serious repercussions – how will the family members cope with the fact that their head of family behaves insanely ... what are the consequences in relation to other families in the same ethnic group... who is to decide in the family ... what to do if there are only daughters in the family ... can daughters decide on behalf of their demented father?

There are potential conflicts in the family, to the extreme that families may even disintegrate. Families are likely to hide the problem as long as possible (this is also valid for many Danish families) as the social consequences can be difficult to deal with. By hiding the problem families follow the basic ethics of honouring the elderly person in the family by, among other things, giving them the care they need in their old age. However, this can lead to problems when the family is then obliged to entrust the public with the care of the family member, whether partly or completely. The family members are liable to be reproached by their own ethnic group for not living up to the above standard that they themselves have set.

Overall, our analyses of the interviews with families who were not from a European cultural background indicated the following problems:

- Lacking knowledge on dementia.

- The social consequences for the family.

- Communication problems.

By contrast, families that are well integrated into Danish society experience dementia in the same way as most Danish families, although the language barrier is still a major problem for these people as well. However, the example below will illustrate the importance of having a bilingual contact person attached to the demented person at institutions for demented people, rather than leaving the task of communication between staff and the demented person assigned to the relatives. Loneliness and a feeling of isolation is the price that a demented person with another language has to pay if bilingual staff are not available. To illustrate the problem of language barrier's and how these can be overcome for elderly demented persons from ethnic minorities, we have included the story of **E** who has a European culture but progressively loses her ability to speak Danish.

The story of E

E came to Denmark in 1926 from Berlin. She came to Denmark to work as a domestic servant for a German family living in Denmark. After a couple of years she met a Swedish man who had also settled in Denmark. They got married and had four children - two boys and two girls. Thus, the children were educated in Denmark.

E was a housewife when her husband died in an industrial accident at the end of the 60s. The pension and insurance left by her husband were sufficient enough for her not to have to work again. In 1985 she moved from her house to a smaller apartment close to her daughter, since she began to have difficulty managing by herself - she had obtained domestic help but this had not 'functioned properly'. The domestic help and E had problems in understanding each other. One of the reasons for this, according to daughter, was her mother's bad Danish. During all the years in Denmark, E had spoken Danish with a strong German accent and this became more pronounced with age. E's condition worsened when she developed Parkinson's disease, making it more difficult to manage alone.

After a couple of years in her new apartment the disease worsened and symptoms of dementia appeared. E's daughter spent nearly all her time looking after her mother and very little time with her own family. The pressure on E's daughter and her family became unbearable, leaving no other choice but to place E in a nursing home. At this point E was speaking something between Danish and German and had great difficulty in understanding Danish. Her dementia symptoms worsened while in the nursing home and eventually communicating with her was only possible in German. However, she was never actually diagnosed as suffering from dementia. Nevertheless, E was lucky that the nursing home realised early on that it was necessary to have a German speaking person who also had an understanding of the German cultural context as E's contact person.

E was now no longer able to speak to her grandchildren or great-grandchildren who had not mastered German, leaving her only able to talk to her daughter and contact person. However, although E's daughter visited her mother frequently she had grown up in Denmark, and though she could speak German she did not always comprehend what E was saying – it was particularly difficult for her to help E with the words and snatches of music when E tried to sing old German songs she remembered from her childhood. However, both E and her daughter benefited from the contact-person who had the German cultural background and therefore knew some of the songs E remembered. She was also aware of the context of the songs – *i.e.* whether they were children's songs, singing games or cabaret songs *etc.*

Overall the co-operation between E, the nursing home, the contact-person and the family was successful for the seven years that E lived in the nursing home. E's daughter said that, as she could not manage to look after her mother herself, she felt safe and content that her mother was in the nursing home. E herself seemed to be happy and satisfied with the arrangement, which she made clear to her children from time to time. In the time E was in the nursing home, she showed no episodes of violence or aggression, although there were disagreements about various things.

Summary. When one compares the story of E with that of Peng's, there is a conspicuous difference as to how well different migrants manage in the Danish Social and Health System even though they all have linguistic and cultural problems in common. In our story about E, the problem is communication with the surroundings.

Conclusion

"*Elderly demented persons from ethnic minority backgrounds encounter many barriers in the Danish Social and Health System, because they communicate their problems in a foreign language or in bad Danish and as a consequence of their different culture*".

Overall our findings highlight a number of issues that concern ethnic minorities with dementia:

(i)   *Knowledge of dementia.* Minority groups' knowledge concerning age and particularly dementia is very limited. The statements from GPs and nurses confirm this: "the family sometimes have difficulty in understanding what has happened to their family member ... the family could have known for a long time that something was amiss but it can be difficult to accept that for example the head of the family suffers from dementia……we have had several cases where we made the diagnosis but the family did not understand what this was all about.... they took the elderly person home and tried with other specialists ... in this way we have had the same elderly person many times through the ward".

114

This lack of knowledge is likely a reflection of the different conception some ethnic minorities have of dementia, although a knowledge of dementia as with other fields is dependent on the level of education a person has. However, it is difficult to get a conception of this when there are cultural and linguistic barriers.

(ii) *Communication.* The lack of a common language (verbal and non-verbal) is of great importance. It is not possible to make the correct diagnosis without a common language. Indeed, this is not possible even with the aid of interpreter since, according to the professionals we interviewed, he/she does not necessarily translate all the fine nuances. Furthermore, the concept of dementia is inextricably linked to the social-cultural context in which the demented person lives. Therefore, communication between the family and the surroundings can be difficult if the family's context differs from the surroundings.

(iii) *Knowledge of culture.* Not understanding and being aware of the socio-cultural context and language of the demented person does not only create barriers to co-operation between the family and institution, but also creates problems in the actual care of the demented person. The importance of having a knowledge of a patients socio-cultural background is clearly shown in the comparison of the stories of E and Peng. Thus, both experience the same problems of communication with the surroundings. However, unlike Peng, E gets a contact-person who speaks her language and knows her socio-cultural background. This enhances the possibility of communicating with the surrounding world and essentially means that the care given to her functions better, is more appropriate and that she attains a real 'existence' – contrary to Peng.

As stated earlier, in Denmark the elderly person suffering from dementia and their family co-operate with the nursing homes to arrange their apartment so that it reflects the environment they came from. We found that the opportunity to do this was only taken up by elderly persons from ethnic minorities that had a cultural background that was close to Danish culture. This suggests that work should be done to extend such opportunities to ethnic minorities with diverse culture's.

The most frequent reason for racist behaviour on behalf of Danes and those from minority groups is often due to a lack of knowledge and respect for the other persons' culture.

Proposals for solving the problems

- It is important that the various ethnic minorities understand what dementia is and what help they are entitled to. This should be done by using pictures and sound rather than through written materials, since there are many elderly persons from these groups who are not good readers (Lindblad and Mølgaard, 1995).

- Since a culture specific method to diagnose elderly people from ethnic minority groups has not been developed, it needs to be seriously considered what diagnosis means. Should it establish whether a person *is* demented or should it establish to *what extent* a person is demented in order to plan the correct care for that person?

- Bilingual staff should be used, or at the very least an interpreter should be employed.

- If possible, ethnic minority dementia patients and their families should be involved in the setting-up of the apartment in the nursing home – *i.e.* as with elderly Danes, the person's own belongings should be used to better reflect the environment the person has previously lived in.

- One should try to form a picture of who the person is and what their life has been like. With this knowledge one is able to create memory workshops, music, songs, smells *etc.* These can be a great help in the care of the elderly person.

4. Participant observations

Demented persons from ethnic minority groups in 'ethnic' nursing homes in Denmark

As mentioned above, few mainstream Danish institutions caring for the elderly have experience of elderly demented people from ethnic minorities. In order to learn about how elderly persons from these groups in Denmark are taken care of we visited an 'ethnic' nursing home with residents of various nationalities, but with a common religious (Jewish) background. The management and the staff of the nursing home were Danish.

Through *observations by participation* that included personal contact with the residents, observing the residents alone, the interaction between residents and care-taking staff, as well as numerous conversations with staff and management, we have an impression of how life is for these elderly demented persons from the largest minority group in Denmark. However, before describing this matter in detail, we would like to present a general description of what we consider to be good care and what aspects of good practice promote the well being of an elderly demented person using a Danish example – **Emily**. Thereafter we would like to present what happens in 'ethnic' nursing homes with the help of some real examples. Finally, a comparative analysis of the quality of care and the importance of ethnicity in connection with the well-being of demented residents will be presented, and some guidelines for what we consider to be necessary to extend good care to elderly demented persons from ethnic minorities.

(i)   Good practice – person centred care[1]

The caregiving *relation.* The caregiving relation is hierarchical since the person who receives care is dependent on the caregiver, because he/she is unable to take care for him/herself. In this sense the receiver of care becomes inferior to the caregiver, who gains some power in the relationship. However, at the same time both are equal, *i.e.* of equal worth because of their common humanity (Martinsen, 1991). Thus, good practice in caregiving is founded on the mutual acceptance of equality between the involved parties. This equality will be acknowledged and confirmed by establishing a dialogue, leading to an agreement on the kind of care that is required and how it should be delivered. Such mutual understanding and agreement will avoid any imbalances and a **relationship** will develop between the caregiver and the patient in which the patient makes use of the expertise of the caregiver, who readily places his/her expertise at the patient's disposal. This is valid whether the caregiver is professional or not – *e.g.* a family member (Scheel, 1995).

The caregiving relation in connection with Alzheimer's disease and similar disorders. It is extremely difficult to create a relationship of human equality, when the patient suffers from Alzheimer's disease or other kinds of dementia. There are a number of reasons for this:

- Demented persons loose cognitive abilities and do not communicate verbally in the same way as other people.

- The social functioning, role and status of a human being in modern society is to a large extent dependent upon a person's cognitive abilities.

- Thus, it is very difficult for modern people, for example caregivers, to really feel and acknowledge the human equality between people with mental disorders and people who function normally in society. You could say, that the caregivers are socialised to feel superior to people with mental disorders[2]

However, there is no reason to believe that people suffering from dementia do not have the same human needs of being seen, heard, understood and confirmed by other people, as any 'normal' human being (Wogn -Henriksen, 1995, p. 136). It is difficult to diminish the imbalance in power that the caregiver has in relation to the patient, and often both professional caregivers and family members relate to demented people without actively involving the demented person in making decisions. Often they do not even try to establish a dialogue with the demented person, not because they are 'bad' people, but simply because they do not believe that a dialogue is possible. This basically means that caregivers give up on trying to establish a caregiving relationship of equal worth based on the common humanity of the caregiver and the demented person.

In order to characterise caregiving as a good, person-centred practice it is necessary to establish a relationship based on a genuine feeling of equal worth and on the basis of a dialogue. No matter what tasks are used in caretaking, and no matter whether the tasks are psychological or practical, the general human need of being acknowledged and confirmed by other human beings has the greatest priority. (Kitwood, 1997; Solem, 1994).

However, a common socio-cultural and linguistic base must be present for the relationship between the demented person and the person who extends the care to function as described above. In this context, ethnic minorities who suffer from dementia are disadvantaged since the staff required to extend to them optimal care, as described above, are rarely available. In this situation the inter-personal imbalance in the caregiving relationship will tend to be exacerbated and there will be a tendency to abandon dialogue in advance.

(ii) To create good practice

The above definition of good practice is stated in very general and abstract terms. What does this definition mean when it comes to the actual caregiving situation, and how does the caregiver fulfil the above general demands?

The caregiver's **personal attitude** and his/her **ability to** communicate have priority among the professional skills needed to create good practice (Feil, 1993; Solem, 1995). This does not mean that general professional knowledge of healthy and unhealthy ageing, of human diseases and disorders, as well as the wide range of practical skills in caregiving are given no priority in the field of taking care of old demented people. On the contrary, these are perhaps even more important in dementia care than in caregiving for other diseases or disorders. However, the difference with dementia care is that demented patients are almost always handicapped with regard to expressing their wishes and demands. Thus, for present purposes we will take for granted that professionals have many of the skills described above and describe good practice from the basis of the caregivers **personal attitude** and **ability to** communicate.

The first questions that arises is how the caregiver identifies which attitude and way of acting gives the demented old person a feeling of human worth, *i.e.* the feeling of being seen, heard, acknowledged, and confirmed, and how the caregiver can evaluate his/her care practice. (Solheim, 1996). However, since every single caregiver has to determine his/her own way of developing a relationship with the demented patient based on equality and dialogue, the task of giving a *prescription* of good practice is impossible. Nevertheless, it is possible to give some **recommendations and guidelines** which are helpful for a caregiver to consider in the caregiving process.

(a) Psychological abilities of demented people
- Demented people cannot hide their feelings.

118

- Dementia does not mean that these people are not able express their emotions.

- Patients with dementia often express themselves clearly, but they may do this in the form of figurative language or actions.

- People with dementia often perceive the meaning of what is said and signalled in their presence.

- Demented people have good intuition.

- Dementia sufferers remember more than other people can directly observe

- These patients often have good reasons for 'strange' verbal articulations or behaviour.

If the caregiver keeps the above psychological abilities of the patient in mind during daily care he/she will realize that the gap between the caregiver and the demented person is not as wide as one might believe. This means that the caregiver is already working on his/her own personal attitudes in a positive and human direction. The following guidelines are helpful when a caregiver wants to transform his/her personal attitude of equal worth as human beings into actions in caregiving

(b) How to interact with the demented person

- Listen seriously when the demented persons talks to you, even if it sounds like nonsense.

- Do not argue with statements made by the demented person. These statements may not be true for you, but they may be valid for the demented person

- Do your utmost to explore what the demented person wants to communicate to you.

- Do not correct the demented person unless this is absolutely necessary to protect him and/or the surroundings, including yourself.

- Do not give too much practical help – remember that things can be done in various ways.

- If you are angry or irritated, tell the demented person – he/she will feel this anyway.

- Do not ask questions to check the memory of the demented person (Amstrup et al., 1987; Feil, 1993).

(c) What to avoid when interacting with the demented person

- Dissociating from the demented person.

- Invalidating the verbal and non-verbal expressions of the demented person.

- Patronising the demented person.

- Being dishonest (Amstrup et al., 1987; Feil 1993).

It is important to remember that many of the points regarding negative reactions by caregivers toward the patient are often unconscious (Wogn-Henriksen, 1995).

(d)   Preparing to interact with the demented person

When the caregiver feels insecure or uncomfortable in interacting with the demented person this is often because the behaviour of the patient causes unpleasant feelings in the caregiver. Therefore, in dementia care it is wise to focus on the baggage of expectations and feelings we often carry with us unwittingly (Wogn-Henriksen, 1995; Kitwood, 1997).   If the caregiver is to acknowledge and confirm the worth and personality of the demented person, it is important that he/she tries to deal with feelings that are uncomfortable. A caregiver may, for example, ask him/herself the following questions:

- Can I stand the fear and anxiety of the demented person, their grief and sadness, or their anger?

- Is it possible that I can share happiness and joy with the demented person?

- Do I tolerate physical contact when there are sexual undercurrents?

- Can I not stand having a rational conversation with the demented person?

- Can I accept the urge for action of the demented person, or handle it when they mess around or shout?

- Can I stand it if the demented person wanders about, perhaps out of our sight?

If the caregiver is able to answer these questions, discovering both what is most pleasant in being with the demented person and what causes the greatest frustrations, it is possible to work consciously on ones own reactions. The purpose of this is not to control your own feelings, but to learn to control how to act upon feelings. Such efforts can be difficult to accomplish alone, and it would be easier if staff members work together under continuous mutual supervision.

(e)   Evaluation of the care giving practice

The British psychologists T. Kitwood and K.Bredin (1992), have developed a series of indicators of a human beings relative well-being in dementia which are useful in evaluating efforts to establish good practice. On a more concrete level of describing good practice, these indicators can be seen as main objectives in the care of old and elderly people suffering from Alzheimer's disease and similar disorders.   These indicators are relevant to all human beings, regardless of ethnicity.

Indicators of relative well-being in dementia:

- The assertion or desire of will.

- The ability to experience and express a range of emotions (both 'positive' and 'negative').

- Initiation of social contact.

- Affectionate warmth.

- Social sensitivity.

- Self respect.

- Acceptance of other dementia sufferers.

- Humour.

- Creativity and self expression.

- Showing evident pleasure.

- Helpfulness.

- Relaxation.

Any care-taking act: serving food, taking care of personal hygiene, stimulation, meeting various psychological needs *etc.*, can be done in a way that promote these indicators of the patient's relative well-being – regardless of the stage of dementia. The caregivers interaction and observations of the demented person along with discussions with colleagues, family members and maybe other people, will make it possible to assess whether the care is promoting one or more of the indicators of relative well-being. If so, then the caregiving practice deserves to be described as a good, person centred practice, though things can always be improved.

(iii)   An example of good, person-centred practice

As mentioned above, it is not possible to give exact prescriptions of what constitutes good practice. The best way to show good practice is to illustrate examples of this in the day to day care of demented people. The example below describes a situation, where the immediate task is psychological, and where the patient and the caregiver are the same nationality. This example has been chosen to clearly show how you can relate your actions to the attitudes, achievements and indicators of relative well-being described above. Throughout the example, the achievements of the caregiver are related to the indicators of relative well-being.

The example is that of an old widow, living alone in a flat. She has some contact with the home care system – daily help with cleaning her flat and doing shopping. She suffers from vascular dementia, for which she has been correctly diagnosed at a psycho-geriatric ward in a Danish hospital.

The story of Emily

An old lady telephoned the community nurse and asked for help because her husband was sitting nude at the dining room table and did not answer her when she talked to him. It was late in the evening, and the old lady had found her husband sitting there while she was preparing to go to bed. When the nurse arrived, the door was opened by a small woman with grey hair, wearing a night-gown and a pair of slippers – Emily kind of smiled and said 'hello'. The nurse introduced herself and said that she arrived because of the telephone call.

The nurse asked: "You called me because of your husband. Should we go and say 'hello' to him?" Emily readily accepted this proposal and took the nurse by the hand to the dining room, and said: "There he is" pointing toward an empty table. The nurse saw that there was obviously nobody sitting at the table, and had prior knowledge that Emily's husband was dead.

But what now, as there was obviously nobody sitting at the table? What is the task?

Here the task of care is to help Emily solve a psychological problem. The nurse began by asking Emily: "Is your husband sitting over there? Could you go over there and show me where he is?" Emily firmly refused to do this. Then the following sequence of events occurred.

Nurse: *"Would you take my hand and follow me to your husband, please?"*

Emily agreed and so they did.

Standing by the table now, Nurse: *"Your husband is sitting here, and he does not answer you?".*

Emily: (in an angry tone) *"Yes, and he has done that before!"*

Nurse (in an angry voice): *"Really! What did you do then?"*

Emily (smiling roguishly): *"I just left him sitting there".*

Nurse (smiling): *"You know what? I think you are a very wise lady".*

Emily (also smiling): *"That was what the physician said, too!"*

Nurse: *"Why don't we leave him there tonight. I can follow you to your bed and help you go sleep?"* Emily agreed. They went to the bedroom together, and Emily lay down in her bed, the nurse put the blanket around her shoulders and asked: *"Do you feel good now?"* When Emily answered *"yes"* (smiling and looking comfortable) the nurse said: *"Then I will leave you now. I hope you will have a good night".* Emily smiled and said: *"Thank you. Nice to meet you".*

What happened here? At first, the nurse tried to work out how serious Emily's fantasy about her husband was. Does Emily suffer from delusions based on dementia or what? Is she psychotic too, or does she have this fantasy because of physical reasons. This cannot be fully explored in this situation. Further observations have to be made, and Emily may have to see her GP or a psycho-geriatric specialist.

By asking Emily to go and point out her husband the nurse gets an idea for what Emily feels. By refusing to go to the table and point her husband out suggests that Emily feels uncomfortable or afraid, so instead the nurse suggests to Emily that they can go together hand in hand. In this way the nurse helps Emily to overcome such feelings and attain a certain degree of

- **Relaxation**

When Emily and the nurse are standing hand in hand by the table, Emily shows no signs of anxiety. Instead she is angry, telling the nurse, that her husband has done this before. When the nurse asks Emily: "What did you do then?", she does not deal with the question of whether the husband is 'real' or not. She respects and accepts that Emily has this fantasy, tries to talk with her about it, and then asks Emily what her own strategy of coping has been in the past. In this way the nurse supports Emily's:

- **Ability to experience and express a range of emotions**

- **Self-respect**

The roguish way in which Emily answers, "I just left him there", tells the nurse that Emily was pleased with her own way of solving the problem, and the nurse tries to support Emily's feeling of being in control and able to handle things by telling Emily that she finds her very wise. This probably promotes:

- **Humour**

- **Creativity and self expression**

- **The assertion or desire of will**

- **Self-respect.**

Emily's way of answering and her seemingly relaxed manner and good mood, tell the nurse that it is appropriate to follow this strategy so that Emily can go to bed and get a good nights sleep. The observations also suggest that Emily's acceptance of the proposal to go to bed is genuine, which is confirmed by the manner in which the two of them go to the bedroom and in the way Emily makes herself comfortable with the pillow and blanket. She is obviously:

■ **Showing evident pleasure**

Finally, Emily says "nice to meet you" in a warm, polite voice and hereby takes the opportunity to show

■ **Social sensitivity**

Evaluation. In the sequence above a dialogue is established on equal terms, as the nurse does not question Emily's description of her problem. Instead, she tries to explore the nature of the problem from a professional point of view and at the same time from Emily's perspective. By following the procedure:

- Showing respect and acknowledgement.

- Asking exploring questions.

- Listening.

- Interpreting verbal and non-verbal expressions.

- Acting accordingly.

- Evaluating her actions on the basis of Emily's reactions.

- Adjusting her actions accordingly.

Emily and the nurse are interacting in a way that promotes many of indicators of relative well-being in dementia described above. Thus it seems fair to suggest that the above example reflects good, person centred practice, since not only is the nurse accepting that Emily is her equal, but she is also continuously evaluating her actions in response to Emily's actions. In this case Kitwood & Bredin's indicators of well-being are fulfilled. However, how successful would this interaction have been if the nurse and Emily were from different socio-cultural and linguistic backgrounds? Is it possible to show respect and acknowledgement or to listen and interpret words and non-verbal actions if one does not have a common verbal and non-verbal lexicon?

Care in 'ethnic' nursing homes in Denmark

"Elderly demented persons from the ethnic minority groups who are gathered in 'ethnic' nursing homes in Denmark suffer serious agonies and have many complicated symptoms in their state of dementia".

'Ethnic' nursing homes in Denmark. In Denmark, there are a few nursing homes which could be called 'ethnic'. However, such homes only exist to the extent that the appropriate food is prepared and served properly, and religious ceremonies, holidays and feasts are celebrated. Thus, both food and religion are taken into consideration

in these nursing homes. As one person from an ethnic minority groups said: "In Denmark it will be important to show consideration for religion and food in taking care of demented elderly from ethnic minority groups".

In the nursing home that we shall focus on the residents are from six different nationalities, whereas both the management and staff are Danish. It is a small nursing home with space for 30 residents. However, only 25 elderly people lived in the nursing home in the period when our observations by participation took place. The Table below shows the spread of nationalities in the home and the number of each.

Nationality of the residents:

Table 6: Nationalities in the nursing home

Nationality of residents	Number of residents
Poland	15
Russia	2
Germany	2
Sweden	1
Norway	1
Denmark	4

Gender. In this nursing home seven residents were men and eighteen women.

Language of the residents. Nine of the 25 residents spoke and understood Danish - however, staff could only have a reasonable conversation with five of these residents as the four Danish-speaking residents suffered from dementia and talked "obscure nonsense".

Diagnosis. Sixteen out of the 25 residents were considered demented by the staff (although few had been through a proper diagnostic procedure). Some of these residents also suffered from physical illnesses but only few had physical handicaps that reduced their mobility.

The distress of the residents in the 'ethnic' nursing homes. Compared to even severely demented Danish residents in Danish nursing homes, where the caregivers are of the same nationality as the residents and where it is possible to establish a dialogue, the old ethnic minority residents in this home were extremely distressed, and showed a lot of troublesome behaviour. There was much more shouting, clutching, restless wandering and aggressive behaviour than what we have seen in comparable Danish nursing homes. For natural reasons we did not observe withdrawal; but we were told by the staff that 6 of the residents almost vegetative - isolated in their bedrooms. Such behaviour has previously been interpreted as symptoms of dementia, but now we know that this is not necessarily the case. This behaviour is likely to be a psychological reaction by dementia patients towards communication and/or other problems in their daily life and environment.

Extreme distress by demented elderly people from a 'non-English speaking background' is described from Australia in 'Cultural diversity and dementia' thus, "Sometimes people think that the distress shown by someone who cannot speak English is due to their dementia, when in fact it is related to their absolute isolation and the fact that they have been deprived of human interaction". The Table below shows the number of residents showing various symptoms which are not necessarily indicative of dementia but may reflect psychological reactions to isolation

Table 7 Complicating symptoms in dementia

Symptom/Behaviour	Number of residents exhibiting this
Shouting	5
Wandering about	5
Grabbing at staff and Co-residents	4
Aggression	5
Apathy	6
None of the above	14

From Table 7 it is apparent that 11 of the 25 residents have serious complications which are not necessarily dementia symptoms, although the 6 residents described as apathetic may actually be in an advanced stage of dementia. That leaves five residents, a fifth of the nursing home's residents, suffering from one or more of the other symptoms/behaviours.

We can put these figures into perspective by comparing them with a typical ward for demented people in a Danish nursing home where 15 residents live. In the Danish home there are no apathetic/vegetating residents, two residents wander about and both can become aggressive if the staff intervene with their wandering. Residents do not shout and none of the residents grab at staff and/or co-residents. Thus, the complicated symptoms described above in the 'ethnic' nursing are relatively rare in a Danish nursing home. The following small vignettes give a description of the behaviour of residents in the 'ethnic' nursing home as a way of demonstrating the complications described above and to give some insight as to why they occur.

Mr. A is immobile and sits in a wheelchair in his room. His wife died recently and he did not go to the funeral as her body was taken back to her country of origin. He has a loud and strong voice and he shouts "mummy" almost constantly when awake, and

126

this resounds around the entire ward. When staff enter his room, he grabs them roughly and it is difficult to get him too let go. The staff cannot calm him by talking to him and after a couple of months of this situation the nursing home called a physician who is a specialist in dementia care and treatment. In the three months that we visited the nursing home there was no change in Mr. A's condition.

Mrs B can walk with the support of one person and has her meals in the common dining room. One day she is having breakfast opposite another lady who is all crumpled up, her eyes closed and food in front of her. Mrs B follows the surroundings with her eyes. An assistant nurse comes walking through the dining room. Mrs B looks at him, says a couple of words in her own language and blows him a kiss. He stops for a short while and says to her in Danish: "Why don't you eat the rest of your food", and then continues walking through the ward. Then Mrs B looks at another assistant nurse who is serving food to another resident and she says something incomprehensible. The assistant nurse answers in a rejecting tone of voice that she should eat her food. Now Mrs B approaches the woman who is dozing opposite her and she utters some indecipherable noises. The other woman does not react. Mrs B does not even expect a reaction but looks down at the table

Mrs C is sitting by a table in the living room. She does not speak Danish. An assistant nurse walks into the room. Mrs C follows her with her eyes and holds up her fingers as if she was holding a cigarette, indicating that she would like. The assistant nurse does not say anything to her but gives her a glass of juice. The assistant nurse leaves the living room but returns shortly with a cigarette that she hands over to Mrs B without a word and hurries on.

Mr. D is sitting in a chair in the living room close to Mrs C. He shouts "hello". The woman who is sitting opposite Mrs B wakes up and also starts shouting "hello". Mr. D shouts "hello" another couple of times but receives no reaction from anyone – he crumbles up and looks as if he is taking a nap.

Mrs E tries to get up from her table in the common dining room. She cannot get up by herself. She tries several times before an assistant nurse comes and helps her to sit in an armchair. Mrs E can get up from the armchair by herself. She gets up and starts walking around the room while speaking, probably in her own language. Neither the co-residents nor the assistant nurse who helped her to get up, react to her words. She starts yelling "hala". More staff members and co-residents enter the room. She approaches them yelling "hala" but nobody reacts. Finally, a trainee arrives who takes her around the waist, says some words to her and takes her for a walk in the living room.

Mrs F is walking down the corridor that leads to the dining room. She knocks at various doors and grabs at everybody, co-residents and staff, who pass her. All the while she is uttering some noises.

Isolation and deprivation of human interaction. In all of the above examples, we meet residents that in one way or another are reaching out for their fellow human beings. Mr. A, Mr. D, the woman sitting opposite Mrs B and Mrs E shout and/or speak very loud. They articulate themselves into 'nothingness', whether they are alone or when other residents and staff are present – i.e. they do not receive any reaction or attention. Mrs C and Mrs F try with eye contact, gestures and grabbing to establish contact with people in their surroundings. Mr. A does the same when the staff visit him in his room. However, the only response they receive is that co-residents and staff evade them. It is such episodes that lead to aggressive behaviour.

These examples from an 'ethnic' nursing home in Denmark clearly demonstrate that there is a lack of good care. The staff make little attempt and lack the possibility to establish proper contact with the residents, because they have a framework at the nursing home that respects only the religious and cultural traditions of the residents. However, they do not have a *common* cultural or linguistic platform with the residents. As with the Australian example above, the staff in this 'ethnic' nursing home presume the behaviour of the residents is to a large extent due to their dementia – not a consequence of linguistic and cultural barriers. Therefore, they do not believe they can help the residents in the situations described above even though from an 'observers' point of view these people are clearly deprived of any human interaction.

The story of Irina - an old demented Russian woman

Before we draw an actual conclusion and make recommendations on how to extend good person-centred care to demented elderly persons from ethnic minorities within the Danish Elderly Care Institutions, Domestic Care System and ordinary nursing homes, we will have a close look at two situations that occur in the interaction between a fictitious person – *Irina* – and others at the nursing home. The two situations will be viewed from the perspective of what we consider to be good person-centred care, using Kitwood and Bredin's indicators of relative well-being to determine whether objectives have been achieved in providing good care. By comparing the case of Irina with examples of good person-centred care (Emily) we would like to reach a conclusion as to whether it is possible to extend good person-centred care to ethnic minorities suffering from dementia. Here we will keep in mind two questions – Is it possible that good care can be given without having knowledge of the language and the cultural context of a person? and; What do things look like from the point of view of an ethnic minority demented person?

Irina has been chosen as an example because she is one of the residents at the 'ethnic' nursing home who apparently neither understands nor speaks Danish. Also, she causes severe problems at the home due to her aggression towards co-residents as well as staff. However, Irina does not exist – she is based on our observations in nursing homes, and the two situations we describe are based upon behaviour we partly observed in daily life at the 'ethnic' nursing home.

Background. Irina suffers from vascular dementia – she has been diagnosed. Until recently she lived at home with her husband, but the burden of taking care of her became too heavy for him, and so she moved into a small nursing home.

Situation 1: human companionship. Irina is sitting at a table, eating breakfast, opposite an old lady who seems to have fallen asleep. A nurse enters the dining room; she was present while Irina received help with her personal hygiene this morning. Another staff member is present. When Irina sees the nurse she says something in Russian to the other staff member, she smiles and points in the direction of the nurse. The nurse returns Irina's smile, goes to her table, sits down beside her, and asks in Danish: "Are you presenting me to .....?". Irina smiles, says something that sounds like the Danish word "yes", and her eyes look joyful and friendly. Irina continues eating. Suddenly she stops, takes her glass of milk and offers it to the nurse. While doing this she says some words. The nurse says in Danish: "Thank you very much, but I think you should drink your milk yourself. I'll go and take something too". When the nurse comes back with a glass of milk of her own, Irina seems at ease, smiling.

After having eaten for a while Irina starts clapping her hands in a certain rhythm, at the same time humming or singing something. The nurse joins her, trying to clap her own hands in the same rhythm, which makes Irina laugh and smile. This happens several times. Between the episodes of clapping hands, Irina says something as well. When she talks, she does not focus on anything or any one. She looks down with a distant look in her eyes. Her tone of voice is low.

About five people are having breakfast in this room. Every time something happens Irina follows this with an interested look in her eyes. After she has done this a few times, the nurse bends towards her, looks her into the eyes and with a smile says in Danish: "I think that you are a curious person?". Irina hears the words, she smiles and laughs. There then follows another episode of rhythmic hand clapping. A man at the next table is interested, and he also frequently laughs and tries with his voice to join Irina in her rhythm. The nurse helps Irina turn towards this man. The two of them now establish a 'rhythmic contact', apparently with joy and well-being. The nurse leaves.

Situation 2: serving dinner for Irina. Dinner is served to most of the residents in a large dining room where 7-8 people, including at least one staff member, sit at each table. Irina is invited to sit down on her chair, but she resists. A staff member tries to persuade her and pushes her softly towards the chair. She becomes angry and the staff member gives in. She leaves the dining room and starts wandering restlessly around. She looks angry and her footsteps are heavy and determined. Another staff member tries to stop her and guide her towards her chair, but again she resists. The staff member does not know what to do to help her eat and drink.

A nurse decides to join Irina in her wandering around. She does not try to stop her. At first, nothing happens. Irina goes on. After a few minutes, however, Irina slows down her footsteps. The nurse is somewhat surprised and slows down her own footsteps. A little later Irina goes to another room in which there are some tables and chairs, but no people. She sits down, and now she is willing to look into the eyes of the nurse, who has followed her and is bending down in order to sit at the same eye level as Irina. Until now no words have been spoken, but at this moment, the nurse says in Danish: "If you want to sit and eat here, where it is quiet, I'll go and get your food". The nurse leaves, anxious to find out if Irina will still be there when she comes back with the food. (the nurse has no reason to believe that Irina might understand some Danish). When she comes back, Irina is still sitting there quietly, and now she accepts her food and starts eating. It is often very difficult to make her accept taking medicine – later the nurse tries this too and Irina agrees and swallows the small pill. At this point Irina's husband comes to visit her – the nurse says "hello" to him and "goodbye" to Irina, before leaving.

What happened here? In practising and evaluating caregiving to demented elderly people there will always be a great deal of interpretation, as you cannot expect verbal feedback that makes sense immediately from the patient. It is difficult to interpret the feelings and actions of demented persons. The ability to do this can to some extent be improved through training and education; but a certain amount of this ability comes with experience in caring for demented patients. Adequate interpretation relies on the common culture, verbal and non-verbal language and knowledge of the patients history. This means that as a caregiver you cannot expect to be able to interpret adequately if you have no knowledge of the patient's culture and linguistic context. This is a huge barrier in understanding and involving oneself with demented persons from ethnic minorities. Therefore, in our analysis of above two situations we shall try to describe what can and cannot be obtained when the two parties belong to different cultures and have a different linguistic context.

Situation 1: human companionship. In this sequence, Irina takes the initiative to communicate by trying to tell another staff member something about the nurse, and Irina engages the nurse in communication by smiling at her. In other words, Irina shows:

- **The ability to experience and express a range of emotions**

- **Initiation of social contact**

And she gets a response, since the nurse goes to her and asks her a question that seems to express an adequate reading of Irina's actions. However, after this episode there is no further communication. Irina eats her breakfast silently, and the nurse stays at the table. The nurse feels no emotional contact either. After a little while Irina takes another initiative, by giving the nurse a glass of milk. Then some verbal exchange takes place, but it would be an overstatement to describe this as successful verbal or non-verbal communication, as one cannot know if Irina understood anything the nurse said. The only valid observation is that Irina smiles when the nurse brings her own glass of milk to the table. However, it is impossible to know whether Irina smiles because her intention is fulfilled, or that she is smiling politely and maybe satisfied with the nurse's attempt to communicate with her.

By contrast, during the rhythmic hand clapping there is a perceptible emotional contact between Irina and the nurse. Again Irina took the initiative, and it was easy for the nurse to join her, as it was based on obvious and clear body language. Still, no verbal communication took place. The communication stays on an emotional level. Irina enjoys her humming and rhythmic hand clapping and shows:

- **Creativity and self expression**

- **Showing evident pleasure**

Thus, whilst Irina receives human companionship, she is given no genuine response to the situation she has created, as the nurse cannot *interpret* what is actually going on – therefore, she is unable to describe and comment on the action and thereby reinforce Irina's act. The nurse shows that she respects Irina's actions, and that it is a pleasure for her to join Irina; but she observes no indicators that would enable her to determine whether Irina has other feelings aside from those of joy and pleasure, i.e. a feeling of self respect in this situation.

This sequence is remarkable in the fact that whenever Irina says something, she does not address her words to anybody – she actually looks down and lowers her voice. Although she is severely demented, she is apparently painfully aware of her extreme communicative isolation from staff members, and presumably also from the other residents.

At the end of this episode, Irina gets involved in the same kind of rhythmic, non-verbal interaction with one of the other residents. They get in contact on the initiative of the nurse, and both Irina and the male resident show.

- **Humour**

- **Social sensitivity**

- **Acceptance of other dementia sufferers**

This initiative is, however, the only time the nurse initiates something in the whole episode; otherwise she has simply reacted. Nevertheless, even in this case the nurse leaves Irina and the male resident to the rhythmic clapping. It is impossible for the nurse to help with the "song" because she has no knowledge of the cultural context in which this song may appear and does not understand the language.

Situation 2: serving dinner for Irina. In this case the staff members have a specific task to accomplish, namely to serve dinner for Irina and see to it that she eats her meal. As stated earlier such a **task** can and should be accomplished within the general framework of good, person-centred care. The first staff member invites Irina to the dinner table, says something in Danish, takes Irina's hand, and gently forces her towards the table – Irina refuses to follow her. As the staff member continues trying to make her sit down, Irina becomes angry. She has an angry expression on her face, leaves the table and starts wandering around taking quick and firm footsteps. Here Irina shows:

- **Ability to experience and express a range of emotions**

Another staff member takes over, and tries by means of the same method to guide Irina to the table, using 'body language' to persuade Irina to give in, sit down, and eat her dinner. When the second staff member tries to stop Irina from leaving the table, the staff member has changed the focus from **person centred** to **task centred** [3], as she is in fact resenting Irina's:

- **Assertion or desire of will**

Thus the staff member is neglecting her person-hood. This is due to the staff members feeling of powerlessness in a situation where it is impossible to establish verbal communication. The feeling of powerlessness leads to an action with an element of power. This is a general phenomenon, which is often seen in taking care of demented elderly people when the demented person resists the actions of the staff. Feeling powerless leads to the use of power. A nurse then tries something else. She does not try to stop Irina. Instead, she offers Irina her companionship in the angry wandering about. After a while it seems as if Irina accepts this offer, as she slows down her pace. A little later Irina goes into another room which is quieter, and sits down. This could be interpreted as a constructive action on Irina's behalf, where she once more expresses "**assertion or desire of will**", as it is likely that Irina feels more comfortable in this room, where she sits down and apparently shows some degree of:

- **Relaxation**

Again this apparent relaxation is a consequence of Irina's own initiative. However, again she is not supported by the nurse, as there is no attempt at verbal communication during the episode – indeed, they do not make eye contact until Irina's angry reaction has abated. At that moment there is an element of emotional contact, in which the nurse takes the opportunity to invite Irina to eat in the place she has chosen herself. In this sequence the nurse tries to show respect for what Irina wishes and does, and she may contribute to a feeling of

■ **Self respect**

However, this is only an interpretation and this should be borne in mind.

Overall, the nurse succeeds in solving the task, as Irina gets her food and her medicine, and she tries to do this using a person centred strategy. She respects and accompanies Irina, and so far, her actions are person centred. However, the mutual contact between Irina and the nurse is diminished by the fact that there is no personal exchange taking place. Although there is a kind of subject-to-subject relationship between the nurse and Irina, based on mutual respect; there is no real contact. Something which one might call a dialogue in body language takes place, and Irina responds to the nurse in a positive way. However, the body language of Irina and the nurse may not have been similar, so important misunderstandings may have arisen – what would have happened in this case then? Even though we are often able to 'read' each others' emotional state in spite of language differences, we must be aware of the fact that many of the non-verbal ways of communication that we take for granted – *e.g.* nod, smile *etc.* – can mean totally different things in certain cultures. Body language is defined by social and cultural contexts, and consequently it is not certain that a smile indicates happiness or a nod means yes. For example, if a Masai nods in response to a question this actually means 'no' rather than 'yes'. Without a common language, interpretation can be very subjective. As a caregiver one feels and is, to some extent, powerless without the spoken language and a common cultural context. If the body language of the caregiver and the demented old person differ, it renders things even more complicated which can lead to serious responses such as aggressive behaviour or withdrawal.

A comparative analysis of the examples from the mainstream and 'ethnic' nursing homes

In the example of Emily the old lady and nurse become involved in a dialogue, where the nurse listens to her, reacts to her story, finds her problems, and helps her solve these problems. Emily uses the experience of the nurse, who lets this happen. Emily is the subject setting the scene, and her initiatives are met. She is seen, heard, accepted and understood, and thus acknowledged as an equal human being. In this example, it is evident that a common language and socio-cultural context is present.

It would not be possible for the nurse to do what she did if the 'common' context had not been there.

In the two situations involving Irina from the 'ethnic' nursing home there is a difference. In Situation 1, Irina had been followed to her seat, and was left alone there with her breakfast. Although Irina was surrounded by other residents, and there were staff in the room serving breakfast for the other residents, she was in fact completely isolated – the lady opposite was asleep and the staff served breakfast to other residents. Irina and the nurse do not establish a dialogue from one human being to another. Irina takes many initiatives. The nurse reacts to the initiatives, but she is not able to interpret what Irina really wants to express, and for that reason she is not able to respond. When Irina talks she looks down and lowers her voice. She talks to nobody. She probably does not expect a reaction to her use of her Russian mother tongue.

In our opinion Irina is seen and heard, but she is absolutely not understood and confirmed as a human being with needs in this situation. She is completely unable to make use of the nurse's professional experience, and it is in this situation impossible for the nurse to let her do so. However, to some extent Irina demonstrates some of the indicators of relative well-being in dementia, but it has to be emphasized that this is not due to the staff, but Irina herself. In this situation, and under these circumstances, it is not possible to conclude that this is an example of good, person centred practice.

Situation 2 is, initially, even worse, since Irina is forced twice to sit down and eat. The staff who serve the food are not trained to solve problems of this kind without verbal communication. The situation could have potentially have become violent. In our interviews with the staff, we were told that Irina had previously become violent in such situations. However, in this case this did not happen because Irina responded to the nurse's attempt to contact her by accompanying her in her wandering and the nurse respected the place Irina finally chose to sit down. With these actions, the nurse may have contributed to Irina's feeling of self-respect. The nurse's actions were person centred, whereas the first attempts to get Irina to sit down to eat were task-centred. Thus, this example shows how **task centred care** was achieved **using a person centred approach**. This conclusion is based upon the fact that Irina shows no resistance to eating when the food is served in the another room. Furthermore, she later accepts her medication when the nurse offers it. Some confidence might have been built between Irina and the nurse, but compared to the Danish example the situation is still very poor. There is almost no human interaction taking place. Irina and the nurse are two isolated individuals, who meet and separate, apparently without leaving any traces behind them, except for the fact that Irina ate her dinner without getting violent that day. This has to be evaluated as a poor result, compared to the obvious feeling of well-being, with which the district nurse leaves Emily in her bed.

Conclusions and Recommendations

Thus, we must conclude that even an 'ethnic' nursing home, where fundamental cultural traditions are maintained, does not necessarily indicate a good quality of life for demented elderly people from ethnic minorities. Human interaction is necessary for all people, irrespective of their nationality or possible diseases. It is difficult to create an emotional or non-verbal dialogue when there is no common socio-cultural platform as a base. Without a common language, it is difficult to establish a common platform to work from.

Although this conclusion gives the impression that nothing can be done in order to improve the care of elderly demented people from ethnic minorities, we would like to temper this viewpoint. Thus, even within the existing framework quite a lot can be done to improve inter-human contact between the client and the care-taking staff if the staff follow the recommendations that are outlined under Good practice – person centred care (see part 4(i) above) under the headings:

- The psychological abilities of demented persons.

- How to interact with demented persons?

- What to avoid in interaction with demented persons?

- How to prepare to interact with demented persons?

These are qualified and elaborated upon under sections 4(ii) and 4(iii) using the example of Emily. These recommendations constitute general guidelines that can be employed in connection with care for demented persons of all nationalities. However, in addition, and with regard to ethnic minorities with dementia, we make the following recommendations to caregivers:

- First focus on the person and then on the task.

- Take the initiative in social interaction as much as possible.

- Always answer when approached by the demented persons, even if they might not understand.

- Pay attention to the same objects and/or phenomena as the demented person.

- Respect the demented person when they refuse something.

- Thoroughly observe and respect the state of mind of the demented person

- Carry out a critical evaluation of your own work performance in a constructive and co-operative way with other colleagues, and be prepared to change working methods.

- Always remain conscious of your attitude as expressed verbally and non-verbally to ensure that racism, whether consciously or unconsciously, does not influence the quality of the care given.

With these recommendations and guidelines, it is possible to attain an equality between the demented patient from an ethnic minority and a caregiver who does not share the same cultural and linguistic context since a subject-subject relationship can develop between the two based on empathy – although in many cases the dialogue would be without words. However, if no attempt at dialogue is made at all, there is a high risk that caregiving becomes task centred with the patient being an object for the actions of the caregiver. This is true, whether the caregiver is a professional or a family member. This point has been confirmed in our observations of Danish care-taking practice in relation to demented elderly people from various ethnic minority groups. To some extent, it was also confirmed in our interviews with professionals and family.

Therefore, interviews, observations and personal experiences in connection with this project emphasize that it is not possible to establish a human dialogue on equal terms, if the involved parties do not share the same verbal language and cultural background and context. Thus, in the long term it is recommended that the framework be established to enable people with dementia from ethnic minorities obtain good person centred care – the necessity being that at least some of the caretakers involved must be aware and understand the patients' culture and are able to a speak their language. A combination of staff members with experience in dementia care and staff with a genuine knowledge of the patients' culture, background, and language will make it possible to establish tolerable life conditions for those elderly people. Nothing less will do.

Notes:

(1) This conception refers to Tom Kitwood: Dementia Reconsidered - the person comes first, Open University Press, Buckingham, 1997.

(2) Tom Kitwood goes as far describing the interaction between the demented person and his/her caregiver using the conception of "malignant social psychology" (Kitwood, 1997, p. 45 pp.).

(3) For a closer description of both the relation and the contradiction between **task centred** and a **person centred** point of departure for care to demented persons, see Kjersti Wogn-Henriksen: "Om at forstå den aldersdemente" i: Kirsti Solheim: Demensguide - holdninger og handlinger i demensomsor- gen, kapitel 4, 1996."

5. Concluding remarks

After having moved from the general context of the individual person to the specific context of care, we would now like to outline the different areas that influence the conditions for elderly persons from ethnic minority groups suffering from dementia:

(i) General social aspects

- Integration policy.
- Social policy.
- Information on dementia and ageing oriented to ethnic minority groups.
- General attitudes in society towards ethnic minorities.
- Research on dementia.

(ii) Possible improvements within the Health and Social System

- Intensification of training staff in dementia care.
- Training of the staff within the Social and Health Sectors with understanding of ethnic minorities.
- Employing both ethnic minority and bilingual staff.
- Improving possibilities for relief for ethnic minority families.

(iii) Conditions necessary for good dementia care

Below we would like to focus on conditions that concern good dementia care which are well known as regards the mainstream – but little is know of these issues regarding ethnic minorities suffering from dementia. Thus, we would recommend that the following conditions are systematically evaluated in these populations:

- The degree of dementia.
- The degree of good care.

However, when it is a matter of demented persons from ethnic minorities, one has additionally to be aware of the following:

- The extent of a common language.
- The amount professional understanding of socio-cultural backgrounds.
- The degree of integration into Danish society, regarding both the patient and his/her family.
- The education and 'knowledge' of the family.

Only when these conditions have been thoroughly studied, would it be possible to start working with the good person centred care that we have described.

We would in particular like to point out conditions that concern the care of the individual:

- 'Narrative methods'.
- Bilingual staff.
- Dementia care.

Conditions that concern the staff and the family:

- Employment of bilingual and ethnic staff.
- Good dementia training.
- Supervision of caretakers.
- Training in cultural understanding for the staff.
- Development of reminiscence workshops.
- Information and training of the family concerning dementia relief

References

Achenbaum A. "Time is the messenger of the Gods": A Gerontologic Metaphor. In: Metaphors of Aging in Science and the Humanities, Editorial Coordinator Donna E. Deutchman, editors G.M. Kenyon, J.E. Birren, J.J.F. Schroots, New York 1991.

Alfredson, Betty Bauer: Förändringsarbete I äldrevården: Utvärdering av personalutbildning inom institutionsbunden och alternativ äldrevård, Lund 1991.

Andersen, K et.al: Prevalence of very mild to severe dementia in Denmark. Acta Neurologica Scandnavica, Munksgaard 1997.

Amstrup, K. et al "Jeg kan ikke mere." – Gerontopsykiatrisk sundheds- og sygepleje, Dansk Sygeplejeråd 1987.

Andersen Kjeld et al   Prevalence of very mild to severe dementia in Denmark, Acta Neurologica Scandinavia, 1997.

Angel, Ronald J. And Jacqueline L. Angel : Mental and Physical Comorbidity Among the Elderly: The Role of Culture and Social Class. In: Handbook on Ethnicity, Aging and Mental Health. Ed.: Deborah K. Padgett, Greenwood Press 1995.

Austveg, Berit: Sundhedssektoren og Indvandrere: Mangfoldighed, sundhed og sygdom. Reitzel 1997.

Ballard, Edna L. et al Recruitment of Black Elderly for Clinical Research Studies of Dementia: The CERAD Experience, The Gerontologist vol 33. No. 4 , p. 561-565, 1993.

Bhabha, Homi K. The Location of Culture, Routledge 1994.

Bjelland, Anne K. Aldring og Identitetskrise, Socialantropologisk skriftserie no. 27, Bergen 1982.

Bofællesskaber for ældre indvandrere – en forundersøgelse. Boligtrivsel I Centrum 1997.

Boligforhold, pleje og omsorg i ti københavnske plejehjem, SBI rapport 283 1997.

Clark, Phillip G. Communication Between Provider and Patient: Values, Biography, and Empowerment in Clinical Practice. Ageing and Society, Vol. 16, part 6, 1996.

Cox, Carol Meeting the Mental Needs of the Caregiver: The Impact of Alzheimer's Disease on Hispanic and African American Families. In: Handbook on Ethnicity, Aging and Mental Health. Ed.: Deborah K. Padgett, Greenwood Press, 1995.

Danmarks Statestik Befolkning og valg. Nr. 6 & 8 København, 1997.

Dinesen Ole Demens: en vejledning for praktiserende læger, Hjerneårets demensarbejdsgruppe, København, 1997.

Dowd, J. J. & V. L. Bengtson "Aging in minority population: An examination of the double Jeopardy hypotesis". Journal of Gerontology 33, 1978.

Ekman Sirkka-Lisa Monolingual and Bilingual Communication Between Patiens with Dementia Diseases and Their Cargivers, Umeå 1993.

Elsass, Peter Sundhedspsykologi, Gyldendal 1992.

Field, D (ed.) Death, Gender and Ethnicity, London 1997.

Feil, Naomi Validering - Hjælp til desorienterede gamle, Hans Reitzels Forlag 1992.

Fischer, Rose, Lucy Qualitative Research as Art and Science. In: Qualitative Methods in Aging Research, ed.: Gubrium, A Sankar, Sage 1994.

Fog, Jette Med samtalen som udgangspunkt: Det kvalitative forskningsinterview, Akademisk forlag 1994

Formidlingscenter Nord Demens til debat, Aalborg 1996.

Gelfand, Donald Reaching and Meeting Ethnic Aged Needs. In: Aging and Ethnicity, Springer Publishing Company, 1994.

Gaunt, David Etnicitet, åldrande och hälse. In: Socialmedicinsk Tidskrift nr. 7 - 8, Stockholm 1996.

Gotfredsen, Kirsten I gode hænder – en temabog om senil demens, Gyldendal Undervisning 1994.

Gunaratnam, Yasmin Culture is not enough: A critique of multi-culturalism in palliative care. In: Death, Gender and Ethnicity. ed.by D. Field,J. Hockey, N. Small, Routledge 1997.

Gubrium, Jaber F., J. A. Holstein Analyzing Talk and Interaction. In: Qualitative Methods in Aging Research, ed.: Gubrium, Jaber F., Andrea Sankar. Sage, 1994.

Gubrium, Jaber F., J. A. Holstein The New Language of Qualitative Method, New York 1997.

Isaksson, Ulla Bogen om E, Hans Reitzels Forlag 1995.

Jackson, James S., Tonni C.Antonucci and Rose C. Gibson Ethnic and Cultural Factors in Research on Aging and Mental Health: A Life-Course Perspective. In: Handbook on Ethnicity, Aging and Metal Health. Ed.: Deborah K. Padgett, Greenwood Press, 1995.

Johnson, M. Dependency and Interdependendency. In: Ed.: Bond, J. and Peter Coleman, Sage 1991.

Kaufman, S. R. In-Depth Interviewing. In: Qualitative Methods in Aging Research, ed.: Gubrium, Jaber F., Andrea Sankar, Sage 1994.

Keith, Jennie et al The Aging Experience: Diversity and Commonality Across Cultures, Sage 1994.

Khader, Naser Ære og Skam, Borgen 1996.

Kitwood, T and Bredin, K (1992) Towards a theory of dementia care: personhood and well-being, Ageing and Society 12: 269-287

Kitwood, Tom: Dementia Reconsidered - the person comes first, Open University Press 1997.

Kratiuk-Wall, Sharon. Chris, Shanley. Kate Russell: Cultural diversity and Dementia, Cera, Center for Education & Research on Ageing, Australia 1997.

Kähler, Runa J. Gammel Kærlighed, København 1996.

Lauridsen Bente Ege Demens – En tikkende omkostningsbombe. Sundhedsøkonomisk analyse af dementssygdomme kap.VI. Københavns Universitet, Økonomisk Institut 1996.

Levin, Jeffery S., ed: Religion in Aging and Health, Sage 1994.

Lindblad P., M. Mølgaard Drøm eller virkelighed, Gerontologisk Inst. 1993.

Lindblad, P., M. Mølgaard "Mine børnebørn går I skole og børnehave – 7 de har ikke tid til mig". I: Samspil, no 2, 1993.

Lindblad, P., M. Mølgaard "Aging and Immigrants". I: Multiculturalism in the Nordic Societies, Tema Nord , Nordisk Råd 1995.

Lindblad P., M. Mølgaard: Hvad med os? Dafolo 1995.

Lindblad, P. et al (ed.) "Elderly People from Minority Groups". A review of the current status of information on research and literature on the topic of elderly from ethnic minority groups in the European Community, Gerontologisk Institut, 1996.

Mace, Nancy L. & Rabins, Peter V. 36 timer i døgnet, Hans Reitzels Forlag 1987.

Madvig, B., M. Schwerdfeger Pårørende til Demente Fortæller, Dafolo 1997.

Markides, K.S. & C.H. Mindel Aging and Ethnicity, Sage 1987.

Martinsen, Kar Omsorg, sykepleie og medisin, Tano 1991.

Mølgaard Mette Jødiske Plejehjem og Ældreboliger i Danmark, Gerontologisk Institut, 1995.

Osborn Averil, D. Willcocks: Making Research Usefull and Usable. In: Researching Social Gerontology, ed. Sheila M. Peace, Sage 1990.

Rowles Graham D., Shulamit Reinharz Qualitative Gerontology: Themes and Challenges. In: Qualitative Gerontology. Ed.: Graham D. Rowles, Shulamit Reinharz. Springer Publishing Company, NY 1988.

Rubinstein Robert, L. In-Depth Interviewing and Structure of its insights. In: Qualitative Gerontology. Ed.: Graham D. Rowles, Shulamit Reinharz, Springer Publishing Company, NY 1988.

Scheel, Merry Elisabeth Interaktionel sygeplejepraksis – Vidensgrundlag, etik og sygepleje, Munksgaard, København 1994.

Snell Helle Hvis bare de forstod. Et bedre netværk for demente I eget hjem, Dafolo 1996.

Small, Neil Death and Difference. In: Death, Gender and Ethnicity, ed.: D. Field, J. Hockey, N. Small, Routledge 1997.

Socialmedicinsk Tidsskrift 1996, häfte 7 – 8: Etnicitet, åldrande och hälse – myter, vård, planering, forskning.

Swane, Christine E. Hverdagen med demens; billeddannelser og hverdagserfaringer i kulturgerontologisk perspektiv, Munksgård 1996.

Swane, Christine E. Glimt i øjet! Udvikling af omsorgen for demente gamle mennesker, Socialministeriets Informations- og Konsulentvirksomhed (SIKON), 1991.

Swane, Christine E. Demens tager tid, Dafolo Forlag, 1993.

Swane, C.E. & H. Kirk Demens i Familien, København 1994.

Solem, Per Erik, m. fl. Demens i psykologisk belysning, Hans Reitzels Forlag 1994.

Solheim, Kirsti   Demensguide – holdninger og handlinger i demensomsorgen, Tano Aschehoug 1996.

Ulholm, Nelly, B. "Der er noget galt", Hans Reitzels Forlag 1990.

Walker Allan   Poverty and Inequality in Old Age. In: Ageing in Society. ed.by J.Bond, P. Coleman, Sage 1990.

Wagner Sørensen, B.   "Bevægelser mellem Grønland og Danmark - Etnisitet, følelser og rationalitet I migrationen. I: Tidsskriftet Antropologi nr. 28, 1993.

Schwitser Klaus-Peter Family Life Cycles: Their Effects on Old People's Family Relations.

In: Aiding and Aging, ed.: John Mogey.

Wenger G. Clare, Said Shahtahmasebi: Variations in Support Networks: Implications for Social Policy. In: Aiding and Aging, ed.: John Mogey, New York 1990.

Wong-Henriksen, Kjersti: IN: Dfemens I psykologisk belysning"; eds. Solem, Per Erik et al., Hans Reizels Forlag, 1995.

France

Omar Samaoli

Acknowledgements

In addition to those acknowledged in the main introduction, I would add the following.

A task of this nature is necessarily the result and work of an entire team. I wish to express my gratitude towards all those who have participated:

Mr. Jaâfar Moumni, Doctor of Biology

Mr. Mehdi Karkouri, Doctor of Medicine, house doctor

Mr. Mare Cohen, Doctor of Medicine, Head of Service

Mr. Sylvain Siboni, Doctor of Psychology, AP-HP (Public Assistance– Paris hospitals)

Mrs Annie Lemorvan, Psychologist, Centre of Gerontology, Fernand Widal Hospital

Mrs Renée Sebag-Lanoe, Doctor of Medicine, Head of Geronotology and Palliative Care Services

Miss Delphine Savouret, Psychologist, A.Binet Centre

Mrs Amel Chaabane, Sociologist

Miss Donatella Montinaro, Interpreter and Project Assistant

The co-ordination of the administrative work and the typing have been taken care of by Mrs Edith Essengue.

I would like to thank the staff and the institutions who agreed to answer our questionnaires. The migrant families who participated are well aware of my support and solidarity.

I extend my friendly gratitude to Mrs. Naina Patel, Mr. Peter Lindblad and Dr. Naheed R. Mirza.

Part 1: The French Profile

1. Ageing in western countries

Ageing is a paradox – according to medical science, ageing is an irreversible bio-physiological fact for all human beings and is a process that begins at birth. However, when assessing the 'human' face of this issue, ageing poses serious social, economic and demographic problems (Leveau & Wihtol de Wenden, 1991).

Today, due to high fertility rates, longer life spans *etc.*, developing societies face new demographic realities. For example, in the Western world significant ageing of the population, non-replacement of some age brackets and increases in life expectancy are incurring economic and social stresses on country institutions (INSEE, 1990). However, these new demographic facts and realities will take on a different dimension and more global implications when considering forecasts for the next century. Developing countries will undoubtedly show the greatest increase in the number of elderly people since the majority of the worlds population live in these countries (Lauzon & Adam, 1996).

In the west where there is an acknowledgement of this demographic revolution, concerns are focused upon the place the elderly occupy in society, and their quality of life (housing, care needs, isolation and resources). The vast majority of elderly people living in the west prefer to continue living at home. The issue of institutionalising elderly people only occurs when they can no longer take care of themselves – *i.e.* they cannot safely perform everyday tasks, when they become a burden to others (family), and/or when the surrounding family network falls apart.

2. The situation in France

Statistics and demographics tend to focus primarily on populations as a whole and only rarely on individuals. Therefore, even in the gerontological world, migrants' ageing has only just started to be noticed due to an increased awareness of the flaws that exist in the care-taking.

On both a regional and, to a degree, national scale, little interest or time has been given to the complexity of migratory movements – sedentary populations, longer stays than intended, large families gathering in the county, and – for our purposes – the future of elderly people in these populations who had initially intended to go back to their countries of origin.

The issue of migrants' health has raised curiosity among scientists and therefore also among public authorities. However, for a very long time only selective pathologies affecting these people were addressed – namely, occupational illnesses and work accidents. However, this was understandable when you consider that the vast majority of migrant workers had notoriously hard jobs in fields such as construction, civil engineering, the iron and steel industry and coal mining. These jobs often caused physical exhaustion and compelled workers to stop working before the legal retirement age.

In the 1970s-1980s, an interest was taken in migrants' psycho-pathological problems (Moussaoui, 1978). Such interest, easily understandable today, concerned fields that were an admixture of health and illness, social adaptation, recognition and the claim for rights – the latter linked to discrimination and prejudice. However, such concerns faced the limited interpretation of professionals and socio-medical law, which made it impossible for migrant's to attain their legitimate rights. This explains the concept/diagnosis that the French call "sinistrose" – a sort of psychosomatic symptom recognized and identified by the psychologists of the time to classify migrants' health complaints – this was the immediate answer, and sometimes the only interpretation given to explain migrants' condition or situation (Comité médical et médico-social d'aide aux migrants, 1977).

In France, the issue of ageing in migrant populations clearly shows the inequalities in the judicial system – elderly people in these communities are deprived of support and services that are usually granted to the indigenous elderly population (Vittoz, 1993). These inequalities occur due to French law, which dictates that some of the services provided for the elderly are dependent upon nationality or territorial conditions – i.e. less privileged people do not have access to many services. Thus, the law itself and the fundamental principles of our Constitution – which forbids discrimination – need to be changed to allow services and financial support to be granted to elderly migrants. More generally, we are concerned by the lack of harmonization in European law concerning ageing, retirement and aid to the elderly – this impinges not only on elderly peoples' social rights, but the unrestricted freedom to move within European boundaries, free and legal access to care, and the possibility to transfer retirement pensions from one country to another.

Thus, from our point of view, this one-year project to which we have dedicated much time, could be seen by some as being a challenge to all the medical and social problems concerning migrants. We take the position that dementia, regardless of its multi-faceted manifestations, is a synonym for suffering. Such suffering includes identification/assessment, interpretation, treatment and care-taking difficulties. Furthermore, these difficulties are all the more poignant when expressed against cultural backgrounds that are not appreciated or considered (Sebag-Lanoë et al., 1993 ; Sebag-Lanoë, 1991).

The CNEOPSA project did not set a common questionnaire for all three countries in the study. We set the broad outlines regarding the information we were each trying to attain, but have not used exactly the same means. Regardless, a comparison of the experiences of France, UK and Denmark regarding the care-taking of elderly migrants with dementia, shows differences in terms of the form of care, and the interest shown by specialist organizations and public authorities in the three countries. This justifies the need to compare and contrast our experiences so as to better organize for the future. Indeed, this project has brought to light new considerations which are important for elderly migrants' gerontological care. Thus, people suffering from Alzheimer's Disease or other forms of dementia are likely to benefit from a multidisciplinary approach and scientific awareness.

In France, geriatric services and establishments are privileged places where physicians are trained and have an interest in this specific area. Therefore, we decided on an approach where we devised a "polyvalent questionnaire" that had to be filled in by physician's, psychologist's and social worker's, with the criteria that each questionnaire was about a dementia care-taking situation. One hundred questionnaires were sent out, targeting hospital physicians as well as physicians who practice privately. Some direct interviews with patients and their families were also done. The interviews focused on the social management of care/suffering for elderly migrants with dementia rather than the clinical dimension.

However, at the outset it must be made clear that contrary to current practice in Denmark and Great-Britain, where to some degree consideration is given to ethnic issues in gerontological care, the medico-social practice in France treats everyone 'equally' with no consideration of the differences in migrants' cultures, beliefs etc. Therefore, in France we were met with both curiosity and skepticism when we announced the CNEOPSA Project.

3. Immigration and ageing in France

The origin of migrants. Migrants in France initially came from a number of countries, including Poland, Italy, Spain, Portugal, the North African countries and, more recently, from other African states (Milza et al., 1995). They were attracted by the prospect of enjoying a higher income, enabling them to meet their own needs as well as that of their families. The migrant worker was often the only source of financial support for the family back home. During this period, immigration was provisional, since these immigrants were bound by social, economic and emotional commitments to their native country. Furthermore, for a long time immigration barely influenced these peoples' personalities, behaviours and reactions, as their whole life was constructed in such a way as not to lose touch with their native country which gave them a strong feeling of belonging somewhere. The following stages in the pattern of migrants coming to France can be distinguished:

- Step one – emigrants came to France in "commanded service", usually sent by their native community; normally a rural community. For example, many

Moroccan families delegated their men to carry out local projects. The emigrants and their families expectation was that in France funds necessary for family or clan projects could be attained.

- Step two – native communities begin to lose control over their emigrants. In spite of the relentlessness monitoring of the emigrant by the peasant community, it did not always succeed in surviving the devastating consequences of emigration.

- Step three – this stage is epitomized by the idea of permanent settlement even if conditions are basic and elementary. Thus, wives enter the family and children are born in immigration – this cycle repeats itself over successive generations.

At this last stage, immigration has been deprived of its meaning and original motivations. As a result the migrant is faced by the issue of legitimacy since neither France nor the native country recognize him/her[1]. Today, we have a better understanding of minority ethnic people who are immigrants in France: on the one hand they are still too close to their culture and life style to be totally integrated into France, whereas on the other hand, they have been transformed by their host societies habits. This middle ground means that migrants face both geographical and cultural boundaries which isolate them from both sides. Many aspects of migrants' situation in France has been previously discussed at length – their arrival in France (Bourdieu & Sayad, 1964), housing conditions (Sayad, 1987 ; Toubon, 1990), health problems and difficulties in integrating (Sebag-Lanoë, 1991 ; Monvalon, 1977).

---

[1] We must bear in mind the fact that work-bound immigration was necessarily not a permanent state ; thus, it was an immigration leading also to people's come backs to their native country.

Demographics

Table 1: Population by age group in France: indigenous and migrant populations

		FRENCH PEOPLE		FOREIGNERS	
	WHOLE		including by acquisition		%
ENTIRE POPULATION	56 634 299	53 026 709	1 777 955	3 607 590	6,4
0 to 14 years old	10 790 081	10 027 237	83 209	762 844	7,1
15 to 24 years old	8 489 963	7 972 469	172 027	517 494	6,1
25 to 34 years old	8 576 290	7 943 130	239 577	633 160	7,4
35 to 54 years old	14 442 372	13 426 769	597 999	1 015 603	7,0
55 to 64 years old	**5 952 394**	**5 648 235**	**284 392**	**304 159**	**5,1**
65 years old and +	**8 360 410**	**8 077 882**	**458 175**	**282 528**	**3,4**
MEN	27 553 788	25 565 524	794 588	1 988 264	7,2
0 to 14 years old	5 527 698	5 138 184	42 285	389 514	7,0
15 to 24 years old	4 319 579	4 051 641	86 772	267 938	6,2
25 to 34 years old	4 266 774	3 939 044	103 429	327 730	7,7
35 to 54 years old	7 279 675	6 612 912	250 976	666 763	9,2
55 to 64 years old	**2 856 860**	**2 660 018**	**127 964**	**196 842**	**6,9**
65 years old and +	**3 305 183**	**3 165 506**	**183 246**	**139 677**	**4,2**
WOMEN	29 080 511	27 461 185	983 367	1 619 326	5,6
0 to 14 years old	5 262 383	4 889 053	40 924	373 330	7,1
15 to 24 years old	4 170 384	3 920 828	85 255	249 556	6,0
25 to 34 years old	4 309 516	4 004 086	136 148	305 430	7,1
35 to 54 years old	7 162 697	6 813 857	347 023	348 840	4,9
55 to 64 years old	**3 095 534**	**2 988 217**	**156 428**	**107 317**	**3,5**
65 years old and +	**5 055 227**	**4 912 376**	**274 929**	**142 851**	**2,8**

Source: Recensement de la population 1990: sondage au 1/20. INSEE

According to the last population census carried out in France, foreigners accounted for 6,4 % of the total population, and 3,4 % of them were 65 years old plus, a trend that shows the importance of ageing amongst migrant groups. Furthermore, of the total number of foreigners in France the percentage that are 65+ is the same as for the indigenous population. However, of the migrants in the 65+ age group, men account for 4,2 % of these, whereas women only account for 2,8 %. This trend does not occur in the general population where approximately equal numbers of men and women make up the 65+ age group. This difference represents a sociological feature of immigration – namely that it was spurred by economic reasons that compelled groups of men, rather than women, to emigrate to France – the imbalance between men and women emigrating to France is probably cultural.

Elderly European and non-European migrants. The following two Tables show the main groups of migrants in France from European and non-European backgrounds of whom significant numbers are elderly (*i.e.* 55+ years of age). Table 2 shows that the main migrants in this elderly category of European origin are Italians, Spaniards and Portuguese. The main non-European groups are of North African descent – namely, Algerian and Moroccan (Table 3). The Tables also show that European migrants exceed those from non-European backgrounds.

Table 2: Elderly migrants of European descent

| | EUROPE | | | | | |
| | Whole | C.E.E. | | | | Polish |
		Whole	Italian	Spanish	Portuguese	
ENTIRE POPULATION	**399 106**	**343 755**	**127 104**	**97 528**	**65 876**	**30 004**
55 to 64 years old	176 703	163 523	52 248	41 756	49 660	3 480
65 years old and	222 403	180 232	74 856	55 772	16 216	26 524
MEN	**205 763**	**181 129**	**65 472**	**49 000**	**36 060**	**10 264**
55 to 64 years old	102 030	94 002	31 448	22 240	28 384	1 864
65 years old and	103 733	87 127	34 024	26 760	7 676	8 400
WOMEN	**193 343**	**162 626**	**61 632**	**48 528**	**29 816**	**19 740**
55 to 64 years old	74 673	69 521	20 800	19 516	21 276	1 616
65 years old and	118 670	93 106	40 832	29 012	8 540	18 124

Source: Recensement de la population 1990: sondage au 1/20. INSEE

Table 3: Elderly migrants of non-European descent

| | AFRICA | | | | | Turkish |
| | WHOLE | HE MAGHR B | | | | |
		Whole	Algerian	Moroccan	Tunisian	
ENTIRE POPULATION	**150 113**	**144 348**	**99 972**	**30 496**	**13 880**	**5 076**
55 to 64 years old	110 200	105 984	72 100	24 120	9 764	3 444
65 years old and	39 913	38 364	27 872	6 376	4 116	1 632
MEN	**112 916**	**109 056**	**75 412**	**23 496**	**10 148**	**3 004**
55 to 64 years old	85 656	82 540	55 048	19 352	8 140	2 300
65 years old and	27 260	26 516	20364	4144	2008	704
WOMEN	**37 197**	**35 292**	**24 560**	**7 000**	**3 732**	**2 072**
55 to 64 years old	24 544	23 444	17 052	4 768	1 624	1 144
65 years old and	12 653	11 848	7508	2232	2108	928

Source: Recensement de la population 1990: sondage au 1/20. INSEE

However, emphasizing the point made above that more men than women make up the migrant population in France, Tables 2 and 3 show that this relative difference in the numbers of elderly male and female migrants only occurs in the non-European but not the European groups. Thus, in Table 3 there are twice to three times as many men in the 55-64 and 65+ age groups than women for all the North African countries. By contrast, Table 2 shows that approximately equal numbers of men and women in these age groups are found in France from all the European countries shown. This imbalance between men and women emigrating to France obviously reflects cultural differences (Tribalat, 1991).

From retirement to old age. Table 4 below emphasizes that the number of elderly migrants remaining in France rather than returning to their native countries is permanent and needs to be addressed. Thus, Table 4 shows the number of people retiring from work in different age brackets. Amongst migrants it is clear that large numbers do not retire until 65-69, 70-74 and even 80+ years of age representing a real and permanent settlement in France; note that the legal age of retirement in France is 60.

Table 4: Age of retirement amongst migrants in France

	WHOLE	FRENCH PEOPLE	including by acquisition	FOREIGNER	%
ENTIRE POPULATION	17 175 267	16 368 212	870 709	807 055	4,7
50 to 54 years old	2 875 004	2 654 108	128 566	220 896	7,7
55 to 59 years old	3 013 106	2 839 133	135 727	173 973	5,8
60 to 64 years old	2 939 288	2 809 102	148 665	130 186	4,4
65 to 69 years old	2 718 210	2 624 780	155 390	93 430	3,4
70 to 74 years old	1 592 482	1 536 121	104 788	56 361	3,5
75 to 79 years old	1 686 603	1 633 522	94013	53081	3,1
80 years old and	2 350 574	2 271 446	103560	79128	3,4
MEN	7 594 312	7 113 781	371 582	480 531	6,3
50 to 54 years old	1 434 250	1 290 038	60 456	144 212	10,1
55 to 59 years old	1 468 935	1 355 470	61 616	113 465	7,7
60 to 64 years old	1 387 925	1 304 548	66 348	83 377	6,0
65 to 69 years old	1 222 263	1 167 019	67 101	55 244	4,5
70 to 74 years old	683 495	652 814	43 396	30 681	4,5
75 to 79 years old	661 281	636 661	35845	24620	3,7
80 years old and	736 163	707 231	36820	28932	3,9
WOMEN	8 875 531	8 573 523	493 779	302 008	3,4
50 to 54 years old	1 440 754	1 364 070	68 110	76 684	5,3
55 to 59 years old	1 544 171	1 483 663	74 111	60 508	3,9
60 to 64 years old	1 551 363	1 504 554	82 317	46 809	3,0
65 to 69 years old	1 495 947	1 457 761	88 289	38 186	2,6
70 to 74 years old	908 987	883 307	61 392	25 680	2,8
75 to 79 years old	1 025 322	996 861	58 168	28 461	2,8
80 years old and	1 614 411	883 307	61 392	25 680	1,6

Source: Recensement de la population 1990: sondage au 1/20. INSEE

Causes of death amongst migrants in France. Although there is a growing interest in Alzheimer's disease in France motivated by developments and improvements in gerontological practice (Moulias, 1996; Ploton, 1994), no statistics on dementia-related deaths amongst the population exists; and this is certainly not the case for migrants.

Table 5: Medical causes of death for men and women who are over 60 years of age in France

	French	The Maghreb Algerian Moroccan Tunisian	E.E.C. Spanish Italian Portuguese	Other nationalities
Infectious and parasitic diseases	6 584	56	100	77
Tumours	112 624	710	2 044	1 205
Endocrine diseases, nutrition, metab., immune troubles	11 998	68	227	142
Blood and hematopoïtc organs diseases	2 312	9	37	28
Mental troubles	10 532	24	148	122
Nervous system and sense organs disease	9 738	35	163	101
Circulatory system diseases	151 653	595	2 705	2 014
Respiratory system diseases	33 795	174	701	487
Digestive system diseases	19 641	85	347	221
Maladies des organes génito-urinaires	6 639	48	110	93
Skin and subcutaneous cellular tissue diseases	2 352	8	23	23
Osteo-articular system diseases, muscles, connective tissue	2 361	10	33	16
Congenital abnormalities	197	1	1	2
No clearly defined symptoms, signs and states	23 989	113	470	442
Extern causes of taumatisms and poisonings	22 886	98	381	304
TOTAL	**417 301**	**2 034**	**7 490**	**5 277**

Source: Service d'Information sur les causes médicales de décès SC - INSERM

Table 5 shows the causes of death amongst both migrants and French people who are over 60 years of age. However, for our purposes this kind of information is not useful as regards Alzheimer's disease. Attempting to match the data on the symptoms shown (tumours, mental troubles, nervous system diseases etc.) which may be closer to our interest in dementia is impossible. Future data needs to more clearly define the cause of death if gerontological understanding is to improve from both a research and practice point of view.

Part 2: Country Practice

Introduction

Immigration as a gerontological issue

Today, speaking about ethnic minority older people in France shows an appreciation not only for these people themselves, but also an appreciation for the in-depth changes that have occurred regarding older peoples' place within the family, an understanding of the relationships that exist between the generations, and the difficulties of urban life. Ultimately, the issue of identity for ethnic minorities is at the fore, since these people now have new social statutory rights in France that are unrelated to elderly peoples' place and role in their native countries.

Difficulties and issues facing aged migrants

Access. In France, when people reach an advanced age, there is nothing odd or surprising in many of them increasingly asking for their retirement pension to be cleared. For ethnic minorities this situation is completely different from that they would have experienced had they returned to their native country. However, today in France ethnic minorities are experiencing inequalities regarding access to some welfare services.

Attitudes. Immigration has also become a gerontological issue, as people are concerned about the issue of elderly people's access to support and services – readjustments in medico-social attitudes are required in dealing with the ethnic minority elderly, particularly when these people enter institutions.

Entering the institutions

Although in France there are some institutions for ethnic minorities which help compensate for the absence of family, in many cases such institutions simply take over from furnished rooms or even workers' foyers where the elderly person can no longer stay, particularly if he/she becomes too much of a burden on other people or is disabled (Kagan, 1996). The presence of elderly migrants' gerontological institutions, although still limited because ageing in these populations has only just become an issue with all its inherent problems and lack of services, are raising concerns about collective and individual issues in care. Amongst these issues is concern about what has become of community solidarity which has stood the test of time – particularly at the time immigration itself. More globally the negative image of ageing and how it is perceived in France needs to be addressed.

As ethnic minorities in France find that the cultural gap is widening between themselves and the models that exist in their native societies, frustrations increase and forecast a series of psycho-pathological problems in these communities which are as yet not discernible. For example, the notion that care for the elderly should be provided for by the family, rather than by external intervention or provision of services, persists among migrants. This adds to the current difficulties in how institutions are perceived by ethnic minorities in France and the fear and guilt associated with contemplating admitting an elderly relative to such an institution. Even when admitted, it is clear that the elderly have great difficulty in integrating in old people's homes or geriatric hospitals. This situation leads to extreme forms of socio-affective, psychological, linguistic and even sensory isolation problems. Such difficulties and problems amongst elderly ethnic minorities in such institutions has raised questions amongst medical staff and social workers. Linguistic problems, and the ensuing difficulties in everyday life situations in these institutions are already the source of many disputes and are, above all, a reflection of the isolation and loneliness of ethnic minorities.

Whether living in institutions or benefiting from residential help, elderly ethnic minority peoples' disarray seems justified as most interventions appear to simply compensate them for their inability to perform daily tasks, often intimate tasks, due to physical frailty. It is apparent that culture's differ in the way that they perceive the body, and therefore the method used to intervene and help elderly minorities needs to consider the issue of intimacy when providing help since these are not necessarily the same between cultures. The legitimacy of intervention needs to be founded on cultural, religious and philosophical grounds.

The absence of any reference to an anthropological identity – *e.g.* elderly peoples' identities for instance – in the training of medical staff, makes it difficult and sometimes even impossible to provide care-taking, ensure communication, support and follow up through the ageing process, regardless of ample good-will and generosity. Gerontology remains convinced of the irreversibility of death at the end of life. Western societies increasingly deprive death of its sense, in order to master the ensuing fear. By contrast, other cultures celebrate it, in its most intimate anthropological features as a natural process linked to a feeling of religious identity. It is in the extremely complex areas where different cultures and realities meet – *i.e.* health, disease, care access, housing, urban integration, social benefits and improvement of services – that integration policies must find their originality. But first, we have to make human diversity in habits, behaviours and even fears understandable and more perceptible. To ignore the person next to you is akin to refusing to accept him/her. This is the reason why our gerontological approach is, above all, dealing with information. If we succeed eventually in reaching our goal we will have participated in providing support to elderly ethnic minority people so that they can grow old and end their life in serenity.

Methodology

The interviewed groups

We have mainly interviewed the following professionals – physicians, psychologists, social workers and health executives. These people were chosen on the basis that they are working with people with dementia, have shown interest in the work and experience the difficulties of caring for ethnic minority people with dementia. Furthermore, the considerable difficulty we have had in interviewing families and the answers they have given us have resulted, to a degree, in us resorting to interviewing these professionals.

Questionnaire

We felt that a questionnaire approach was an appropriate method of attaining the information we required since it allowed the professional's to express their own point of view concerning practice and patients – with no influence. However, we were also aware of the lack of time many of these people have and therefore their reluctance to agree to direct interviews which take considerably more time. Finally, this method allowed us to generate a large sample size which would otherwise have been impossible considering the time constraints under which we had to work.

As stated earlier we in France concentrated on the social management of care/suffering. Therefore our questionnaire concentrated on the following aspects:

*   life conditions;
*   financial means;
*   quality of family network;
*   institutionalization conditions;
*   reliance;
*   care-taking and needs.

The questionnaire consisted of 33 questions and approximately 100 copies were sent too professionals – of these, seventy questionnaires were completed and returned. Others were either not used due to insufficient data or never returned. Overall the number of people refusing to participate was low. A copy of the questionnaire can be found in Appendix 2.

Other contacts

As well as contacting professionals involved in the care of people with dementia, we also directly contacted either patients or their relatives. Although their statements and comments do not appear in our results section below they have contributed to the overall sentiments and conclusions derived from this study.

Results

The results are presented as a series of Tables followed by pie-charts for clarification.

Tables

Table 6: The life style of demented ethnic minorities

Life style	Alone with husband/wife	33,33%
	Long term beds service	22,22%
	Alone at home	22,22%
	Structure specialized in the care of people suffering from Alzheimer's Disease	11,11%
	At home with people other than	11,11%
	Total	**100,00%**

As an adjunct to Table 6, we are aware that there is a tendency for elderly migrant's with or without dementia to be institutionalized or put into contact with medial and social services much more readily than non-migrant's.

Table 7 Welfare

Welfare	Yes	100,00%
Back-up health cover	No	88,89%
	Yes	11,11%
	Total	**100,00%**
Housing allowance	No	66,67%
	Yes	33,33%
	Total	**100,00%**
Family allowance	No	100,00%
Free medical aid	No	77,78%
	Yes	22,22%
	Total	**100,00%**
Additional allowance	No	66,67%
	Yes	33,33%
	Total	**100,00%**
Allowance for disabled adults	No	100,00%
Minimum income	No	77,78%
	Yes	11,11%
	No answer	11,11%
	Total	**100,00%**

Table 8: Physical condition

Capabilities		without help	minimum help	partial help	complete help
	to stand up	55,56%	11,11%	22,22%	11,11%
	to lie down	33,33%	33,33%	22,22%	11,11%
	to wash oneself		33,33%	22,22%	44,44%
	to get dressed	11,11%	22,22%	22,22%	44,44%
	to eat alone	33,33%	33,33%	22,22%	11,11%
	to move within a limited area	44,44%	33,33%	11,11%	11,11%
	to move outside a limited area	22,22%		22,22%	55,56%
	to take the prescribed drugs		11,11%		88,89%

Table 9: Cognitive abilities

Capabilities		Capable	With difficulties	Unable
	Notion of time		11,11%	88,89%
	Notion of space		66,67%	33,33%
	Memory of recent events		11,11%	88,89%
	Memory of past events	11,11%	55,56%	33,33%
	Understanding of simple or	33,33%	55,56%	11,11%
	Oral communication	44,44%	44,44%	11,11%
	Written communication		11,11%	88,89%
	Reasoning capacities		55,56%	44,44%

Table 10: Additional psychiatric and behavioural problems

Behaviour		Never	From time to time	Frequently	Always
	Wandering about	44,44%	33,33%	22,22%	
	Aggressiveness	44,44%	44,44%	11,11%	
	Insomnia	44,44%	33,33%	22,22%	
	Reluctant to be help	11,11%	44,44%	11,11%	33,33%
	Delirious ideas / Hallucinations	44,44%	44,44%	11,11%	
	Aimless activity	44,44%	22,22%	22,22%	11,11%
	Sadness	33,33%	33,33%	33,33%	
	Running away	77,78%	22,22%		

Table 11: Degree of support from family and social services

Main support	Husband/Wife	16,67%
	Child	50,00%
	Professional	16,67%
	Caretaker	16,67%
	Total	**100,00%**
	Home curer	16,67%
	Physiotherapist	16,67%
	Housekeeper	16,67%
	Social worker	16,67%
Main support is helped	Yes	50,00%
	No	50,00%
	Total	**100,00%**
If yes from whom	Professional	100,00%
Regular consultation	Geriatric service	50,00%
	No consultation	50,00%
	Total	**100,00%**
Frequent visits to	Day-care hospital	50,00%
	No visit	33,33%
	Day-care reception centre	16,67%
	Total	**100,00%**

Table 12: Reasons for a lack of support from professionals/care centres

Reasons for	o resorting to a professional	No need	Excessive cost	Patient's refusal
	Psychiatrist	50,00%		16,67%
	Nurse			16,67%
	Home physiotherapist	66,67%		
	Speech therapist	66,67%		
	Housekeeper/duty nurse		16,67%	33,33%
	Specialized hospital service	33,33%		
	Day-care reception centre		16,67%	16,67%
	Temporary housing structure	33,33%	16,67%	

Table 13: The social and medical needs of demented ethnic minorities

Needs	Housekeeping	50,00%
	Laundry	50,00%
	Home care	50,00%
	Distribution of meals	50,00%
	Voluntary /Duty nurse	33,33%
	Physician's visit at home	33,33%
	Telephone	16,67%
Practitioners	Physician	66,67%
	Social worker	22,22%
	Psychologist	11,11%
	Total	**100,00%**
Diagnostical difficulties	No	66,67%
	Yes	33,33%
	Total	**100,00%**

Table 14: Problems in care-taking

Specific problems	Yes	100,00%
If yes, they concern	language	77,78%
	relations	77,78%
	social and cultural habits	55,56%
	future	11,11%
	family	11,11%

Table 15 The benefit of specific care-taking techniques

Specific care-taking	Yes	77,78%
	No	22,22%
	Total	**100,00%**

Table 16: Examples of specific care-taking methods employed and problems

Some additional	- Arab-speaking assistant
elements	- Conformity with diet habits
	- Day-hospital, mainly manual activities
	- Specific care-taking in day-hospital with activities, presence of helper during meals, break isolation
	- The staff has had to learn a few words in Arab (to eat, to drink, to stop, hi, thank you...)
	- Lack of helpers speaking the patient's language and knowing the patient's cultural habits. These helpers could regularly be asked to intervene
	- Lack of list of professionals entitled to help us draw up a diagnosis for an ethnic minority patient
	- Day-care centre (5 days out of 7), problems on week ends, no care-taking

Pie charts

The charts below are intended to clarify some of the information given in the Tables above. However, they additionally give information on the cohort of elderly ethnic minority people in question – *i.e.* gender, age, origin *etc.* The numbers following the title of each pie-chart indicate the number of the question in the questionnaire (see Appendix 2).

Chart 1

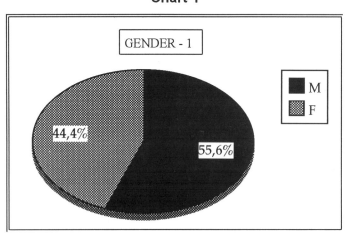

Chart 2

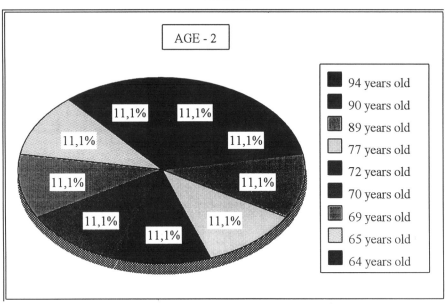

Chart 3

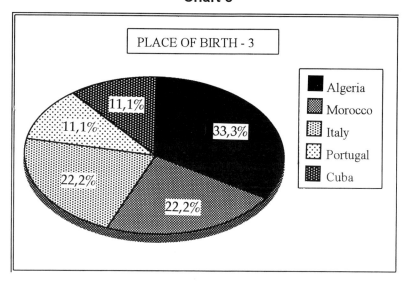

PLACE OF BIRTH - 3

- ■ Algeria
- ▦ Morocco
- ▨ Italy
- ▦ Portugal
- ▦ Cuba

33,3%
22,2%
22,2%
11,1%
11,1%

Chart 4

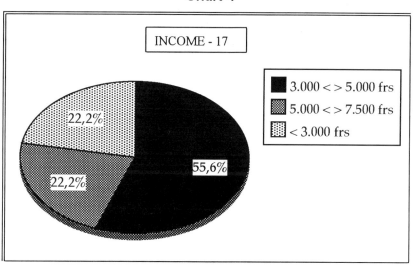

INCOME - 17

- ■ 3.000 < > 5.000 frs
- ▦ 5.000 < > 7.500 frs
- ▦ < 3.000 frs

55,6%
22,2%
22,2%

Chart 5

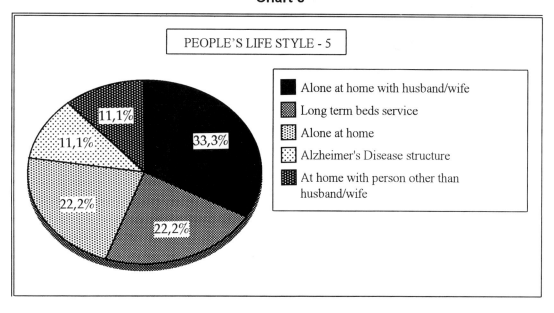

PEOPLE'S LIFE STYLE - 5

- ■ Alone at home with husband/wife
- ▦ Long term beds service
- ▨ Alone at home
- ▦ Alzheimer's Disease structure
- ▦ At home with person other than husband/wife

33,3%
22,2%
22,2%
11,1%
11,1%

Chart 6

PEOPLE'S NEED FOR SERVICES - 28

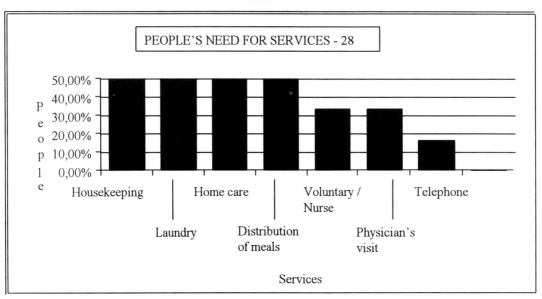

Chart 7

DATE OF FIRST SYMPTOMS - 18

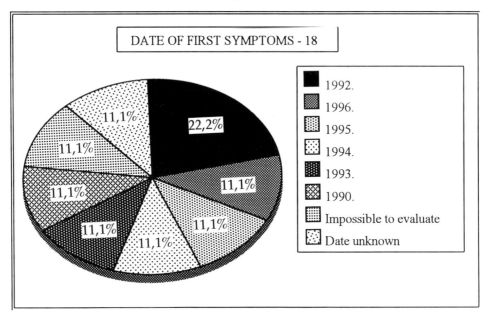

Chart 8

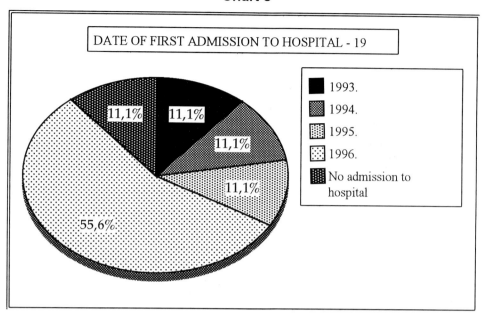

DATE OF FIRST ADMISSION TO HOSPITAL - 19

- ■ 1993.
- ▦ 1994.
- ▧ 1995.
- ▨ 1996.
- ▦ No admission to hospital

11,1% 11,1% 11,1% 11,1% 55,6%

Chart 9

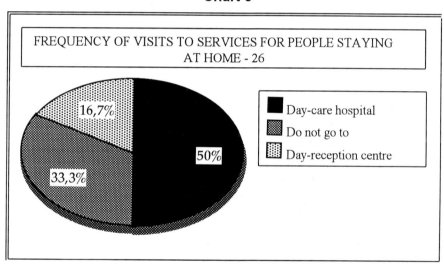

FREQUENCY OF VISITS TO SERVICES FOR PEOPLE STAYING AT HOME - 26

- ■ Day-care hospital
- ▦ Do not go to
- ▧ Day-reception centre

16,7% 50% 33,3%

Chart 10

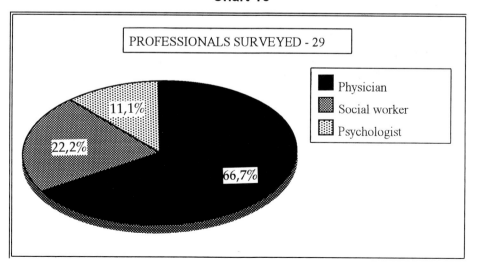

PROFESSIONALS SURVEYED - 29

- ■ Physician
- ▦ Social worker
- ▧ Psychologist

11,1% 22,2% 66,7%

Chart 11

SPECIFIC PROBLEMS - 32

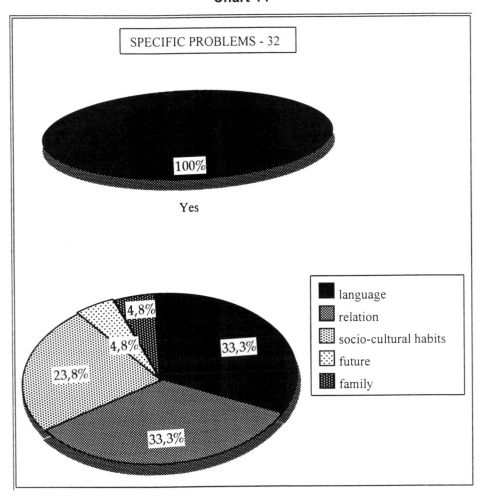

100%

Yes

language
relation
socio-cultural habits
future
family

4,8%
4,8%
23,8%
33,3%
33,3%

Chart 12

SPECIFIC CARE-TAKING - 33

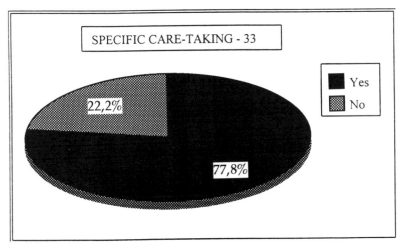

Yes
No

22,2%
77,8%

Discussion

From the answers that we have received it is not easy to directly discuss what good and bad practice are because of the way that gerontological care-taking for immigrant origin/immigrant populations is organized. The data that we have generated does, however, demonstrate notable problems in the care of elderly ethnic minorities which care staff themselves have noted (Table 14), and the needs and improvements which are required for optimization of care-taking of these people (Table 13 and Chart 6). However, in addition we feel it necessary to highlight the fact that in addition to these peoples' suffering, the suffering experienced by the carers, often family members (Table 11), is also worthy of mention since the two are likely to be linked.

On issues of attaining help from social services for performing daily tasks such as housekeeping, hygiene, care *etc.* we find that the ethnic minority elderly have access to these services. However, we also find that those elderly ethnic minority people who live at home (66,6%), 11,1% of whom live alone, have considerable financial difficulties (Chart 4) which makes it difficult to attain the support they require (Table 11).

With regard to those elderly ethnic minorities living in institutions we find that like their counterparts living at home, the services they receive and the quality of these services are strongly influenced by other factors – namely, the language of communication and the role of relatives. Without an ability to communicate sufficiently care or care-taking is almost impossible. Furthermore, care-taking needs to take into consideration socio-cultural habits which include intimacy spheres (body, washing *etc.*) as well as identity spheres (dietary habits, religious practices *etc.*). These issues scored highly as "*specific problems*" (Chart 11) amongst those we interviewed. However, these findings on care issues are in complete contrast to the issue of diagnosis, where 66,6% of professionals interviewed said that this was not a problem with regard to ethnic minority elders (Table 13).

Recommendations

In considering our recommendations it is apparent that a majority of care-taking staff (77,78%) felt that specific care-taking techniques were required with ethnic minority elders (Chart 12). Based partly on the examples of specific care-taking techniques used by professionals (Table 16), we recommend that the following aspects and problems be considered in the care of ethnic minority older people with dementia:

- a choice of helpers speaking the patients' language;
- respect for dietary habits;
- care-taking in day-hospitals;
- an adaptation of activities to better reflect the elderly ethnic persons culture;

- re-socialization and approval of community activities;

- a need for anthropological enrichment in the training of care staff;

- poor structure of support;

- absence of stop-over organizations when day centres are closed.

The profile of recommendations and problems in relation to these peoples' needs should be assessed according to their social situation. Thus, as our survey shows, some ethnic minority older people live at home without attending a day centre, others live at home and frequently visit these centres, whereas others live in institutions (Table 6/Chart 5 and Table 11). Any recommendations made also need to consider these social conditions. Such considerations also highlight the fact that, regardless of whether they require greater anthropological sensitivity, not all people's needs are the same in terms of access to services, helpers or care-taking – again emphasizing the specificity of the care-taking approach for ethnic minorities discussed above.

Optimizing care

From the outset we have expressed our reluctance to draw a definitive line between what is considered good and bad practice in diagnostic methods, care and care-taking. We rather prefer to highlight the short-comings of current practice. It is clear that carers enforce their practice with good faith and focus on their egalitarian characteristics. For example, hygiene procedures in care are rightly considered good practice to maintain comfortable conditions. However, according to anthropological and different cultural beliefs such procedures can be perceived as inadequate. The same applies to diagnostic criteria where physical symptoms are not considered as equally important as verbal responses, identification of materials or reasoning. Physical symptoms may actually aid in determining whether an ethnic minority older person has dementia, since language and cultural barriers exist between the patient and professional who is likely to use the standard techniques/tests to ascertain whether a person has dementia. The psychiatric and psychological methods currently used in gerontology may therefore not be appropriate for ethnic minorities. We do not question the scientific knowledge in this area, but rather encourage science to carefully adapt and acclimatize to all things a human being can express as a result of his/her cultural diversity. However, the introduction of anthropological training to better reflect our cultural diversity amongst medical, professional and care-taking staff is still only a recent development that has yet to been validated.

Conclusion

From the information we have generated we think that the following elements should be focused on when considering care-taking of ethnic minority older persons with dementia:

- The language issue is of prime importance. Carers should be able to read or understand the patient's language. We are only asking that foreign language courses become part of training for professional medical and social services staff.

- Cordial "friendship", meaning the right of the patient to be visited whilst being cared for in an institution. The training of carers needs to consider the importance of visits from relations for ethnic minority older people. Family visits and religious requirements, just like the right to visit, are sometimes contrary to the strict rules concerning the need for keeping quiet in such institutions. Dietary habits for patients in institutions must also be carefully considered by care staff. In many cases the problem of ethnic minority older people 'breaking the rules' stems from a lack of consideration of some of these concerns.

- Intimacy – we have already stressed the importance of respect for the way in which some ethnic minority older people perceive their body. We are underlining this issue because of the firm conviction from experience in the field, that washing and getting dressed, aesthetic care and body hygiene can affect the integrity of the patient's body. Integrity here means an awareness of the limits that define the boundary where intimacy starts – i.e. what it is possible to touch or to show and what is impossible or is seen as over-stepping the boundary.

- Religion is a fundamental factor in care and care-taking relations. Attention to religious practices needs to be considered in gerontology and other fields. The religious aspect takes on a specific meaning when we think about more intimate problems involved with mortuary preparation, burial and other similar circumstances.

If how we understand our counterparts is a necessity to us, just as it is fundamental for us to master cultural differences and gaps, then the factors above should be perceived as a means by which to improve care for the whole, as well as selectively identify specific populations.

References

Association France Alzheimer Et Troubles Apparentes. (1995). *Enquête nationale auprès des familles ayant en charge un parent atteint de la maladie d'Alzheimer ou de troubles apparentés.* Paris : France Alzheimer.

Badou, G. (1989). *Les nouveaux vieux.* Belfond : Ed. Le Pré aux Clercs.

Berr, C. (1993). Les facteurs de risques des démences séniles : Les données épidémiologiques, *La Revue du Praticien - Médecine Générale, 227.*

Bourdieu, P. & Sayad, A. (1964). *Le déracinement : la crise de l'agriculture traditionnelle en Algérie.* Paris : Editions de Minuit.

Caillet, H. *et al.* (1994). L'imagerie dans la maladie d'Alzheimer : Une aide de plus en plus performante pour le diagnostic, *La Revue du Praticien – Médecine Générale, 243.*

Cohen. D. & Eisdorfer, C. (1989). *Alzheimer : le long crépuscule : Un guide de ressources pour toute la famille.* Québec : Les éditions de l'Homme.

Comite Medical Et Medico-Social Díaide Aux Migrants. (1977). *La santé des migrants.* Paris : Droit et liberté.

Ethier, S. (1996). *L'ABC de la maladie d'Alzheimer.* Québec : Editions du Méridien.

Guillet, P. (1994). Prise en charge à domicile des patients atteints de la maladie d'Alzheimer: Quel rôle pour le généraliste ?, *La Revue du Praticien - Médecine Générale, 257.*

Hebert, A. (1997). *Précis pratique de gériatrie.* Canada : EDISEM.

Hervy, M. P. *et al.* (1994). Le traitement de la maladie d'Alzheimer : Tenter de rendre la vie du patient et de son entourage supportable, *La Revue du Praticien – Médecine Générale, 245.*

INSEE. (1993). *La société française : données sociales 1993.* Paris : INSEE.

Joly, D. (1991). Minorités ethniques et politiques locales en Grande-Bretagne. In : D.

Lapeyronnie (Ed), *Les politiques locales d'intégration des minorités immigrées en Europe et aux Etats-Unis* (pp. 345-387). Paris : ADRI.

Kagan, Y. (1996). *Dictionnaire de pratique gérontologique.* Paris : Frison-Roche.

Khosravi, M. (1995). *La vie quotidienne du malade d'Alzheimer : Guide pratique.* Paris : Doin Editeurs.

Lacoste-Dujardin, C. (1985). *Des mères contre les femmes : maternité et patriarcat au Maghreb.* Paris : La découverte.

Lacoste, C. & Lacoste, Y. (1991). *L'état du Maghreb.* Paris : La Découverte.

Lacoste-Dujardin, C. (1991). Le statut ambigu des vieilles femmes en Kabylie, *Hommes et Migrations, 1140,* 34-36.

Lacoste-Dujardin, C. (1992). *Yasmina et les autres de Nanterre et d'ailleurs : filles de parents maghrébins en France.* Paris : La découverte.

Lamour, Y. (1993). Etiologie de la maladie d'Alzheimer : Une moisson de découvertes permet de mieux comprendre l'origine de la maladie, *La Revue du Praticien - Médecine Générale, 231.*

Lapeyronnie, D. (1991). *Les politiques locales d'intégration des minorités immigrées en Europe et aux Etats-Unis.* Paris : ADRI.

Lauzon, S. & Adam, E. (1996). *La personne âgée et ses besoins : Interventions infirmières.* Paris : Editions Seli Arslan.

Leveau, R. & Wihtol de Wenden, C. (1991). *Modes d'insertion des populations de culture islamique dans le système politique français.* Paris : MIRE.

Lequin, Y. (1988). *La mosaïque France : Histoire des étrangers et de l'immigration en France.* Paris : Larousse.

Maisondieu, J. (1989). *Le crépuscule de la raison.* Paris : Bayard.

Messy, J. (1994). *La personne âgée n'existe pas.* Paris : Rivages.

Milza, P. *et al.* (1995). *L'intégration italienne en France : Un siècle de présence italienne dans trois régions françaises (1880-1980).* Bruxelles : Editions Complexe.

Montani, C. (1995). *La maladie d'Alzheimer : "Quand le psyché s'égare".* Paris : L'Harmattan.

Moulias, R. & Meaume, S. (1996). Réflexions sur l'éthique et la recherche en gérontologie et en gériatrie, *Gérontologie, 98,* 15-22.

Moulias, R. *et al.* (1997). Transférer des malades âgés : problèmes déontologiques et éthiques, *Gérontologie, 104,* 19-25.

Moussaoui, D. (1978). *Psychopathologie des maghrébins migrants en France. Mémoire pour le C.E.S. de psychiatrie.* Paris : Université René Descartes.

Nuland, S. B. (1994). *Mourir : Réflexions sur le dernier chapitre de la vie.* Paris : Interéditions.

Pageot, J. C. (1989). *Vieillesse société et démence.* Canada : Méridien gérontologie.

Ploton, L. (1994). La communication avec les déments : L'échange est possible et peut être favorisé, *La Revue du Praticien - Médecine Générale, 249.*

Ploton, L. (1995). *La personne âgée : son accompagnement médical et psychologique et la question de la démence.* Lyon : Chronique sociale.

Ploton, L. (1996). *Maladie d'Alzheimer : A l'écoute d'un langage.* Lyon : Chronique sociale.

Roach, M. (1991). *Alzheimer : Un autre nom pour la folie.* Besançon : La Manufacture.

Samaoli, O. (1989). Immigrés d'hier, vieux d'aujourd'hui : la vieillesse des maghrébins en France, *Gérontologie, 70.*

Samaoli, O. (1991). L'immigration à l'épreuve de la vieillesse en France, *AGORA, 17.*

Samaoli, O. (1991). Les immigrés dans la vieillesse, *Gérontologie et société, 56,* 165-173.

Samaoli, O. (1996). Vieillir dans l'immigration, *Nouvelle Tribune, 12,* 37-39.

Samaoli, O. (1997). *Recherche-action en Seine-Saint-Denis, Montreuil – Bobigny – La Courneuve : Etat de santé, conditions de vie et risques de dépendance des migrants âgés.* Paris : OGMF.

Sayad (Abdelmalek) *et al.* (1987). *L'immigration en France : le choc des cultures. Actes du colloque, Problèmes de culture posés en France par le phénomène des migrations récentes, mai 1984.* Lyon : Centre Thomas More.

Sebag-Lanoe, R. (1986). *Mourir accompagné.* Paris : Ed. Desclée de Brouwer.

Sebag-Lanoe, R. (1991). De la douleur de mourir loin de sa terre, *Hommes et Migrations, 1140,* 14-18.

Sebag-Lanoe, R. (1992). *Soigner le grand âge.* Paris : Ed. Desclée de Brouwer.

Sebag-Lanoe, R. & Feteanu, D. (1993). Quand évoquer la maladie d'Alzheimer ? Un diagnostic essentiellement clinique à n'affirmer qu'avec prudence, *La Revue du Praticien - Médecine Générale, 235.*

Sebag-Lanoe, R. & Feteanu, D. (1994). Prise en charge institutionnelle des patients atteints de la maladie d'Alzheimer, *La Revue du Praticien - Médecine Générale, 251.*

Sebag-Lanoe, R. & Feteanu, D. (1994). Formules de prise en charge des patients atteints de la maladie d'Alzheimer, *La Revue du Praticien - Médecine Générale, 268.*

Sebag-Lanoe, R. (1997). *Vieillir en bonne santé.* Paris : Ed. Desclée de Brouwer.

SOINS. (1992) Vieillissement cérébral et soins aux personnes âgées, *Soins, 567.*

Toubon, J. C. & Messamah, K. (1990). *Centralité immigrée : le quartier de la Goutte d'Or. Dynamiques d'un espace pluri-ethnique : succession, compétition, cohabitation.* Paris : L'Harmattan & CIEMI.

Tribalat, M. (1991). *Cent ans d'immigration, étrangers d'hier français d'aujourd'hui: Apport démographique, dynamique familiale et économique de l'immigration étrangère.* Paris : INED & PUF.

UNASSAD & FNG. (1988). *Détérioration et démence au quotidien : les malades, les familles, les services, les professionnels à domicile. Actes du colloque, 4 et 5 mars 1988, Paris.* Paris : UNASSAD & FNG.

Vittoz, H. (1993). Un accès au droit commun difficile, *Ecarts d'Identité, 64,* 14-16.

Wihtol De Wenden, C. (1991). La politique migratoire française et les immigrés âgés, *Hommes et Migrations, 1140,* 6-8.

Conclusion

As explained in the Introduction, the purpose of our project was to initially establish the state of research, practice and developments in each of our three countries regarding minority ethnic older people with dementia/Alzheimer's Disease. This purpose has been achieved in the Country Profile and Country Practice sections for the UK, Denmark and France. The information that was collated and analysed resulted in specific proposals, and indicated both differences and similarities between the three countries. The proposals should aid planning in the management of care by family carers, professional carers, organisations and policy makers. All too often developments occur on an ad hoc basis in the area of ethnicity and health. However in this area of mental health of minority ethnic older people with dementia, the information and proposals we make suggest that this situation need no longer persist. The potential exists to develop a logical and comprehensive strategy in the care of these people. It only requires government policy direction, commitment and resources by relevant authorities to nurture and strengthen the work that is already in progress. Why? - to develop and manage appropriate care to minority ethnic older people with dementia.

1. Country Profile

The country profiles portrayed the situation of minority ethnic older people with dementia in the UK, Denmark and France. The information gathered did not allow us to distinguish between Alzheimer's diseases and other dementia disorders so the general term of dementia was adopted.

The Epidemiological profile of dementia/Alzheimer's disease

We established the general profile of minority ethnic older people, but emphasized the diversity of people who come within this broad term in our three countries. So the profiles of minority ethnic older people varies between the three countries in terms of size, socio-economic position, settlement period, their background as a refugees, colonialism or economic migration and how the issue of minorities and discrimination is regarded in the three countries. However, all three countries commonly share the basic fact that minority ethnic older people are ageing, and that they are a permanent settlement in these countries whether their families are with them or not.

When we considered the information available on dementia we found several gaps:

First, it was not possible to obtain adequate statistics on minority ethnic older people with dementia. Instead we made an estimate on the basis of general figures.

Secondly information on the prevalence and the number of persons with dementia was available in all our three countries but the figures were not classified by ethnicity. Thirdly, the cost of dementia care was known in all three countries but again none was to be found for minority ethnic groups. Finally, information on research, print material and developments were not available in Denmark and France although some existed in the UK. The lack of research information, print material and developments was found amongst both organisations engaged in the care of minority ethnic older people as well as in the field of Psychiatry.

In short, it can be said from our country profile sections that for the three countries examined, much information exists on dementia among the older people from majority ethnic groups (*e.g.* in terms of statistics, economic costs, research, organisations engaged and psychiatry and social care areas). However, there is paucity of information and developments when we consider minority ethnic older people with dementia. It can therefore be concluded that the current knowledge and practice base in this area is low or non-existent across in all three countries.

Recommendation 1: The gaps identified need to be remedied through a planned programme of research and practice developments. The country profiles should be regarded as providing a baseline of information on the knowledge on dementia care for minority ethnic older people. This should be used to plan and assess future progress.

2. Country Practice: the experience of various groups providing care

(i) The family in connection with dementia

Socio-economically. We can discern country differences in this area. For the British and French minority ethnic families, the biggest problem is one of obtaining access to care and welfare system. By contrast, in Denmark these barriers are not as marked. The difference in Denmark may reflect better socio-economic position of families – *i.e.* in the context of housing and the general entitlement to benefits.

Knowledge on dementia. In all three countries, the general knowledge of the minority ethnic families on dementia was considered to be poor. However in the UK print information and video resources were developed to provide information to various minority ethnic groups.

Contact with the social care and benefit system. The available knowledge among minority ethnic families on how to access the system and the various forms of assistance was considered to be low.

Barriers. Apart from socio-economic barriers experienced by the minority ethnic families particularly in the UK and France, knowledge, communication, professional-interaction, prevalence of racism, organisational and cultural – care barriers were noted in all three countries. Amongst families from minority ethnic backgrounds there existed a 'concept barrier': by this we mean that dementia/Alzheimer's disease was conceived not as a disease but as 'an act of God' or the result of normal ageing. Finally even when perceived as a disease there was a tendency to 'hide' to avoid social labelling.

Recommendation 2: In view of the above issues, we think the following need to be considered to improve the situation of minority ethnic older people with dementia and their family carers:

- *a planned information and educational support programme on dementia/ Alzheimer's Disease and Care using different modes of communication;*

- *a concerted action to improve the socio-economic conditions including improved access to welfare entitlements;*

- *professional care and support to the family carers;*

(ii) The Professional Carers

General Practitioners. In the UK, France and Denmark the general practitioner is the first point of contact in the care and health system for a person with dementia and/or their family carer. In all three countries, there is no mandatory training which equips general practitioners to deal effectively with the medical problems faced by minority ethnic older people with dementia. General practitioners expressed the view that it was difficult for them to 'catch'/identify minority ethnic older persons with dementia. The key problems can be summarised as:

- communication – when the same language is not shared it is clearly very difficult to establish understanding. But even when the same language is shared 'medical-phobia' amongst patients or the inability of the general practitioner to communicate adequately renders medical visits ineffective;

- lack of information and understanding of cultural background, and differences in how the patient and the General Practitioner view the disease;

- difficulties with dementia tests applicable to different minority ethnic groups;

- difficulties in explaining to the family carer what dementia entails.

Recommendation 3: It is therefore necessary build up expertise in research, education and training (e.g. skill development) to enable General Practitioners to effectively address the medical problems – within an appropriate cultural, linguistic and anti-discriminatory framework - of minority ethnic older people with dementia.

Psychogeriatricians. Based on our pilot study method for each country we established the following information from specialists in geriatrics:

- all tests are culturally specific to the majority ethnic groups;

- at present there are no accepted cultural-specific tests which can be used with minority ethnic patients;

- It is extremely difficult to work through an interpreter in connection with dementia tests (e.g. Denmark);

- there is a large element of error in reaching diagnostic decisions – e.g. in distinguishing between mild and severe dementia;

- there are difficulties experienced in explaining information and communicating with family carers.

Recommendation 4: It is essential that appropriate diagnostic instruments are developed and that information to family carers is better explained and communicated.

Social and Health Care Professionals. In all three countries we found that professional social and health care staff expressed different attitudes to what constituted 'good practice' regarding care of minority ethnic older persons with dementia. However, the following similarities in problems were noted by all three countries:

- a gap in knowledge of the cultural context of the minority ethnic older people with dementia;

- a gap in both knowledge and competence as regards language and cultural communication;

- problems experienced in working with the families/carers;

- problems experienced in specialist/professional knowledge regarding dementia and forms of appropriate care;

- problems in resources and policy commitment to the area;

- problems in providing person-centred care on the basis of the above.

We found that most noted difference in our country practice in this area was in the level and attention given to the general area of ethnicity. This is in turn helped to create specific focus on minority ethnic older people with dementia. The issue of appropriate care in task-centred care or person-centred care also emerged.

Recommendation 5: Social and Health Care professionals are providing an essential service to the care of people with dementia. It is necessary to build up expertise in research, education and training (e.g. skill development) to enable Social and Health Care Professionals to provide effective person centred care to minority ethnic older people with dementia. within an appropriate cultural, linguistic, spiritual and anti-discriminatory framework. There is an urgent need to support the development of specialist staff on dementia from minority ethnic groups.

(iii) *Minority Ethnic Organisations*

The UK study focused on the capacity and potential of these groups to meet the needs of minority ethnic older people with dementia. It is clear from their country conclusion that such organisations are attempting to meet the challenges as best as they can. They are in a critical position responding to the needs of people with dementia from various minority ethnic groups, but they are also in close contact with mainstream authorities and organisations such as Alzheimer's Disease Society.

These organizations suggested that the level of knowledge, specialist staff, resource materials, infra-structure support and capital and human resources were problems that needed to be considered to meet the increasing demands from family carers of persons with dementia.

Recommendation 6: *Given the low knowledge and practice base concerning care to minority ethnic older people with dementia, the urgency to develop specialist resources is made apparent. A satellite model is recommended where investment in a few identified minority ethnic organisations in the UK would be an appropriate step in developing necessary specialist resources. Moreover, this satellite model could potentially be adapted in Denmark and France where minority ethnic associations do exist but not in the same form as in the UK.*

Majority ethnic organisations like the Alzheimer's Disease Society have an important role to play, but this should be in association with minority ethnic organisations who are already engaged in a specialist role which caters for various minority ethnic older people.

Summary

Whether a 'wonder pill' for Alzheimer's disease and other forms of dementia is found, one thing is certain: person oriented care is currently the only possible 'treatment' that allows the life of older people with dementia to be tolerable. Appropriate, adequate and accessible care to minority ethnic older people with dementia is critical if people of all ethnic backgrounds are to lead a dignified life. All respondents in the three countries stressed this as reflected in their agreement with Kitwood and Bredin's list of quality of life indicators(1992)).

We must emphasise that our recommendations are not fanciful ideas created from dreams or a vacuum. They emerge from an informed basis by identifying and studying three specific modalities important in the care of minority ethnic older people with dementia – *i.e.* the Country Practice in the three countries. In addition, the country profiles provide a sound baseline against which future developments should be planned and measured, and recommendations made as in the case of our country practices which are summarised in this conclusion.

As we approach the year 2000 the presence of minority ethnic older people in the UK, Denmark and France will become even more significant in terms of numbers. It therefore becomes even more critical that this work and the work of others cited in this book are not seen as a 'fad' or a one-off development.

This book provides a real possibility for a comprehensive approach in better care for people with dementia from minority ethnic backgrounds: as stated earlier, developments in this area, may also lead to spin-offs that benefit **all** people with dementia.

Thus, in both policy and practice the choice is,
> (a) whether to disregard the information and proposals presented here
> or
> (b) whether to seriously work with such material to help change the current low
> (or non-existent) knowledge and development base,
if we desire improved dementia care for *all.*

Appendix 1 – The general context: Alzheimer's Disease

(by Dr Naheed Mirza for the CNEOPSA team)

What is Alzheimer's disease?

"Alzheimer's disease is the most prevalent late-onset neurodegenerative disorder of unknown origin" (Lamy, 1994). It is characterised clinically by deficits in cognitive function, including memory, thinking, orientation, comprehension, calculation, learning capacity, language and judgement. However, these cognitive deficits occur together with a number of heterogeneous psychiatric and non-cognitive behavioural disorders which vary in their severity and frequency over time (Herrmann *et al.*, 1996). They include psychosis, delusions, depression, aggression/agitation, personality changes, decreased motivation/ arousal, excessive eating, sexual disinhibition, misrecognition, rage behaviour, anxiousness, sleep disturbances and incontinence. Finally, there are a whole host of neurological deficits including, impairments in reflex responses (*e.g.* snout reflex, grasp reflex), myoclonus, and extrapyramidal signs, which all lead to a loss or difficulty in controlling movement. The disease is insidious in onset and early signs include untidiness, forgetfulness, transient confusion, restlessness interspersed with bouts of lethargy. The various stages of the disease can be defined in a number of ways. For example, mild dementia when independent living is possible but there are deficits in work and social interaction, moderate dementia when symptoms increase in severity and to live independently some supervision is required, and finally severe dementia when the person needs constant supervision (White *et al.*, 1995; see also Herrmann *et al.*, 1996). The disease typically occurs at ages greater than 65 years, but in a small number of cases people develop the disease as young as in their 40-50's.

Diagnosis of probable Alzheimer's disease

Alzheimer's disease can only be diagnosed with certainty by post-mortem study of brain tissue (see below). Otherwise it is diagnosed using various diagnostic criteria set out in the Diagnostic and Statistical Manual of Mental Disorders (DSM-IV) of the American Psychiatric Association or the diagnostic research criteria set jointly by the National Institute of Neurological and Communicative Disorders and Stroke (NINCDS) and the Alzheimer's Disease and Related Disorders Association (ADRDA). DSM-IV is aimed at dementia generally whereas NINCDS/ADRDA is specifically for Alzheimer's disease. The World Health Organization (WHO) has a classification of dementia based upon many of the criteria set out in DSM-IV known as the International Classification of Diseases (ICD-10). However, the criteria set by these bodies can only test for the *probability* of Alzheimer's disease, since by their very the classical tangles seen in neuronal cells in Alzheimer's disease brain (Iqbal *et al.*, 1991).

How do you get Alzheimer's disease?

Although the largest single risk factor is old age, it is likely that Alzheimer's disease is a disease with polyetiology including genetic (see above), environmental toxins chronic infections and metabolic abnormalities. Examples in these categories include, family history of Alzheimer's disease, Parkinson's disease and Down's syndrome, exposure to aluminium and occupational toxins, head trauma, thyroid disease, alcohol and diet. Other putative risk factors include depression, low education and non-smoking (Fratiglioni, 1993). However, can all these different etiologies lead to the same pathology – *i.e.* tangles (abnormal *tau*) and plaques (β-amyloid), neuronal cell loss, synapse abnormalities and all the associated biochemical and physiological changes? Recent studies have tried to integrate all this leading some to claim that Alzheimer's is a disease of many etiologies but one pathology (*e.g.* Hardy, 1992).

What treatment is available?

As stated Alzheimer's disease patients suffer not only from cognitive deficits but also associated psychiatric problems, behavioural disturbances and neurological impairments. There are both pharmacological and non-pharmacological treatments available. Non-pharmacological treatment includes "behavioural management, environmental modifications, interventions using sound and light, social interaction groups and other psychosocial activities" (Herrmann *et al.*, 1996). Pharmacological treatment at present is aimed at treating either the cognitive deficits, the behavioural symptoms, or slowing the rate of decline (Schneider, 1994).

To date only the drug tacrine (cognex®) has been licensed in the US and France to treat cognitive deficits in Alzheimer's disease, although this drug is only effective in a subpopulation of patients due to side-effects – namely hepatoxicity (Knapp et *al.*, 1994). Recently a derivative of this compound with an improved side-effect profile, Aricept®, was launched in the UK (Giacobini and Cuadra, 1994). Most other drugs given as medication to Alzheimer's disease patients are used to treat the psychiatric and behavioural disorder's – these cause the greatest burden to caregivers (Whitehouse and Voci, 1995). Commonly used drugs include antispychotics, anticonvulsants, β-blockers and benzodiazepine**s** to alleviate aggression, agitation, disruptive behaviour, catastrophic reactions (strong emotional responses) and hallucinations. Various classes of antidepressants have also been used, not only to alleviate depression and anxiety but also to help manage agitation and aggression. However, many of these treatments have side-effects such as sedation, social withdrawal, hypotension, falls, dizziness, confusion, motor imapirments and even cognitive impairment (*e.g.* benzodiazepines), hence exacerbating some of the actual symptoms of the disease itself (Herrmann *et al.*, 1996). More recently, estrogen therapy, anti-inflammatory drugs, selegeline and Vitamin E have all been suggested as potentially useful avenues of research in developing drugs to treat and/or prevent Alzheimer's disease (see NIH, Progress report on Alzheimer's disease, 1997).

References for Appendix 1

Burns, A. (1993). Accuracy of clinical diagnosis of Alzheimer's Disease. *Alzheimer's Review.* **2(1)**: 25-28.

Fratiglioni, L., Ahlbom, A., Viitanen, M., Winblad, B. (1993). Risk factors for late-onset Alzheimer's disease: a population-based, case-control study. *Ann-Neurol.* **33(3)**: 258-66.

Gauthier, S., Feldman, H., Mohr, E. (1994). Minimal efficacy criteria for medications in Alzheimer's Disease. In: *Alzheimer Disease: Therapeutic Strategies.* Eds. Giacobini, E. Becker, R. Birkhäuser, Boston. pp 431-35.

Giacobin, E., Cuadra, G. (1994). Second and third generation cholinesterase inhibitors: from preclinical studies to clinical efficay. In: *Alzheimer Disease: Therapeutic Strategies.* Eds. Giacobini, E; Becker, R. Birkhäuser, Boston. pp 155-171

Goate, A., Chartier-Harlin, M. C., Mullan, M., Brown, J., Crawford, F., Fidani, L., Giuffra, L., Haynes, A., Irving, N., James, L., et-al (1991). Segregation of a missense mutation in the amyloid precursor protein gene with familial Alzheimer's disease. *Nature.* **349**: 704-6.

Hardy, J. (1992). Alzheimer's Disease: many aetiologies; one pathogenesis. In: *Heterogeneity of Alzheimers Disease.* Eds. Boller, F. Springer-Verlag, Berlin.

Herrmann, N., Lanctôt, K. L., Naranjo, C. A. (1996). Behavioural disorders in demented elderly patients. *CNS Drugs.* **6(4)**: 280-300.

Iqbal, K., Grundke-Iqbal, I. (1991). Ubiquitination and abnormal phosphorylation of paired helical filaments in Alzheimer's disease. *Mol-Neurobiol.* **5(2-4)**: 399-410.

Knapp, M. J., Knopman, D. S., Solomon, P. R., Pendlebury, W. W., Davis, C. S., Gracon, S. I. (1994). A 30-week randomized controlled trial of high-dose tacrine in patients with Alzheimer's disease. *JAMA.* **271(13)**: 1023-4.

Lamy, P. P. (1994). The role of cholinesterase inhibitors in Alzheimer's Disease. *CNS Drugs.* **1(2)**: 146-65.

Nordberg, A. (1994). Use of PET technique to monitor effect of drugs in Alzheimer's Disease treatment. In: *Alzheimer Disease: Therapeutic Strategies.* Eds. Giacobini, E., Becker, R. Birkhäuser, Boston. pp 405-13

Progress report on Alzheimer's disease (1997). National Institute on Aging/National Institutes of Health. U.S. Department of Health and Human Services, NIH Publication No. 97-4014.

Saunders, A. M., Schmader, K., Breitner, J. C., Benson, M. D., Brown, W. T., Goldfarb, L., Goldgaber, D., Manwaring, M. G., Szymanski, M .H., McCown, N. et-al (1993). Apolipoprotein E epsilon 4 allele distributions in late-onset Alzheimer's disease and in other amyloid-forming diseases. *Lancet.* **342**: 710-1.

Schneider, L. S. (1994). Pharmacologic management of agitation and depression in dementia. In: *Alzheimer Disease: Therapeutic Strategies.* Eds. Giacobini, E., Becker, R. Birkhäuser, Boston. pp 343-48.

Terry, R. D. (1994). Neuropathological changes in Alzheimer disease. *Prog-Brain-Res.* **101**: 383-90

White, H., Clipp, E. C., Hanlon, J. T., Schmader, K. (1995). The role of the caregiver in the drug treatment of dementia. *CNS Drugs.* 4(1): 58-67.

Whitehouse, P. J., Voci, J. (1995). Therapeutic trials in Alzheimer's disease. *Curr-Opin Neurol.* **8(4)**:275-8

Appendix 2 – The EMEE Declaration on dementia/Alzheimer's Disease 1997

The European Minority Ethnic Elderly (EMEE) group made this specific addition to their general declaration on Care and Welfare. The EMEE group wish this declaration to be used specifically in dementia related work.

The Declaration states:

> *The problem of dementia among the elderly from minority ethnic groups is of great concern to us. We therefore urge policymakers and professionals in national countries and at the European Commission to positively look into its implications for the care and welfare of people affected.*

> *We also urge caution on the possibility of scientific racism creeping into research studies examining dementia among minority ethnic older people in Europe.*

– EMEE Declaration at the European Network on Ageing and Ethnicity (ENAE) Euro-seminar, 19-21 December 1997, Masstricht, Netherlands.